The Best
One-Act Plays
of
1963–64

Also edited by Hugh Miller

THE BEST ONE-ACT PLAYS OF 1952–53
THE BEST ONE-ACT PLAYS OF 1956–57
THE BEST ONE-ACT PLAYS OF 1958–59
THE BEST ONE-ACT PLAYS OF 1960–61

The Best
One-Act Plays
of
1963–64

Selected by
HUGH MILLER

GEORGE G. HARRAP & CO. LTD
London Toronto Wellington Sydney

The reproduction of any part of these plays by a duplicating machine, or in any other way, whether the reproductions are to be sold or not, is a violation of the copyright law.

First published in Great Britain 1965
by GEORGE G. HARRAP & CO. LTD
182 High Holborn, London, W.C.1

© *as stated at the opening of each play*

*Composed in Intertype Baskerville type and printed by
Western Printing Services Ltd., Bristol
Made in Great Britain*

Preface

Ten years ago, in a foreword to a volume in this series, the editor anticipated hopefully that the widening field of television would assure a plentiful supply of one-act plays. He was mistaken, for in the event, television series and serials which exploit personalities have proved much more popular than short plays. That faulty guess just shows that the public taste in drama may be as capricious as the housewife's choice in detergents.

But any predictions connected with theatre are perilous. The anxious manager, well aware of this, must wonder if he will ever have the benefit of a computer to remove some of the fearful risks from show business. How pleasant to be able to feed into a machine fixed data relating to author, plot, settings, direction, production, and operating costs, together with such complex variables as stars' popularity-rating and all the familiar risks—war, weather, Court mourning, national debt, moon's phase on opening night, etc., and then only have to sit back and listen to the apparatus announcing the precise distance between the management and the bankruptcy court. And how relieved an editor would be if he were similarly guided in the choice of plays, all guaranteed to have international appeal.

But the fact is that the theatre will always remain beyond the most sophisticated calculation, just as in the past it has constantly eluded the estimates of dramaturgic pundits and the astutest men of show business.

To the compiler of the present collection, schooled on the stages of London and New York, the first certainty in the theatre is uncertainty, and the second is the public's constant appetite for plays not entirely new but just different. A well-varied collection is of course the ideal, but if it be thoroughly representative of prevailing styles the danger is that conservative readers may be baffled by the extremes of Absurdism or fearful of Theatre-in-Hell drama, just as devotees of *avant-garde* movements may be bored by any form of traditionalism or works which fail to crash the sense barrier. But that is not the only reason why plays of certain *genres* do not appear.

Theatre history provides monotonously recurring examples of the fickleness of fashion. To-day's most fetching piece of millinery becomes to-morrow's old hat. One is indeed entitled to wonder whether even now the fine feathers of John Osborne and Nigel Dennis are not drooping a little. But of course a good play remains a good play though its theme and technique may be outmoded.

For example, Parisian audiences applauded Émile Zola, when, dedicated to realism, he set out to kick the attitudinizing romantic hero off the stage, and bring the sweating face of life before the footlights. *Thérèse Raquin* made history, and it remains a good play, but it is very doubtful whether the latest form of realism—the Theatre of Cruelty—will prove to have the staying-power of Zola's work.

The only history so far made by the new drama, crammed with gore and evisceration, has been to put the Grand Guignol out of business.

In the field of Absurdism, where tragedy apes farce and characters without human roots resign themselves to being unable to communicate with one another, that distinguished man of the American Theatre, Harold Clurman, considers that all Absurdism's premises are perversions and fortifies the editor's own feeling. Anyhow, Absurdism in this book would look like the Twist in an international ballroom dancing contest.

Leaving now the exclusions and coming to the chosen works, Peter Coke shows wit and skill in a comedy where a pair of tricksters play an elegant diamond-cut-diamond game in Italy. Helena Jones sets her play in Roman walls destroyed by the uncivilized, while Michael Walker's drama is about a modern wall which the civilized hope to destroy. Michael Dines' theme is malfeasance at a Spanish frontier-post, and *Genius Loci*, a quatercentenary celebration play, is appropriately set in Stratford-on-Avon. Bryan Stocks with his nine frolic muses invites beautiful young actresses to exchange kitchen-sink drama for the waters of Hippocrene, and an intriguing play by Ella Adkins is about a greying little woman, and shows again how a strong character springs from a strong story.

H.M.

Contents

	PAGE
IN CONFIDENCE *Peter Coke*	9
THE WALL *Michael Walker*	37
AFTER ROME *Helena Jones*	63
GENIUS LOCI *Sagittarius*	93
REPORT FROM CONTREROS *Michael Dines*	115
TROUBLE ON HELICON *Bryan Stocks*	133
THE DEVIL'S LIMELIGHT *Ella Adkins*	149

In Confidence

By Peter Coke

© 1964 *by Peter Coke*
All Rights Reserved

Adapted from the television production, which was presented by Associated Rediffusion, and directed by Bill Hitchcock, on June 21, 1963, with the following cast of characters:

(in the order of their appearance)

TOUT	*Massimo Pietrobon*
ANGELA FAIRBOURNE	*Vivien Merchant*
COL. EDWARD APLIN	*Dennis Price*
PHILLIPO	*Leon Auerbach*
GIUSEPPE	*Gabor Baraker*

Applications regarding amateur performances of this play should be addressed to Messrs Samuel French, Ltd, 26 Southampton Street, Strand, London, W.C.2, or Samuel French Inc., 25 West 45th Street, New York.

In Confidence

SCENE: *A small, sunny square in an unfashionable part of Venice. Morning.*

About half the area seen is occupied by the terrace of the "Trattoria del Ponte," screened from the square by wood lattice-work, creepers, and flowers and shrubs in tubs and pots. It has two or three small tables with gay umbrellas. At the back is the dark entrance—through a bead curtain—to the restaurant.

When the curtain rises the stage is empty. Faint music comes from a radio inside the restaurant. ANGELA FAIRBOURNE, *gay, enchanting, middle-aged, comes into the square badgered by a slick, poorly dressed young* TOUT, *who speaks with a strong Italian accent.*

TOUT. You want nice gondola, *signora*?

ANGELA. No, thank you very much.

TOUT. Very good gondola—take you all place, cheap price.

ANGELA. Not to-day, thank you.

TOUT. To-day I show you famous sights of Venice, yes?

ANGELA. No. [*Hopefully.*] Good-bye.

TOUT. You want to see glass factory?

ANGELA. No, thank you. [*More firmly.*] Good-bye.

TOUT. I show you nice place to eat?

ANGELA. No!

TOUT. Very clean; speak English; give pot of tea.

ANGELA [*losing patience*]. I don't want a pot of tea!

TOUT. What you want then?

ANGELA. I want you to leave me alone.

TOUT. But I like you, *signora*. [*Touching her.*] You very pretty lady.

ANGELA. I'm getting a very angry lady.

TOUT. Pretty lady with pretty clothes, pretty rings, and—[*with his eye on it*] pretty bag.

ANGELA [*waving him away with her hand*]. Go away. *Via!*

TOUT. I *via* if you open bag, pretty lady.

ANGELA. If you don't go away immediately I'll call a—[*glancing around anxiously*] some one.

TOUT [*trying a new tack—whining*]. I have very ill Mama, signora.

ANGELA. Then go to her.

TOUT [*dramatically*]. She die if not eat. [*He puts his hand on her bag.*] Open bag; give me money buy food.

ANGELA [*frightened*]. Take your hand off my bag.

TOUT. Just thousand lire, pretty lady.

ANGELA. No. Go away.

TOUT. When you give money.

ANGELA [*really alarmed*]. I'm not going to. Go away—please.

TOUT [*threateningly*]. *Signora*, if you not give money——

[*He is interrupted by a bellowed stream of invective which comes from the door of the restaurant.*

COLONEL [*off; bellowing*]. *Senta ragazzo! Lasci quella donna in pace o chiamo la Polizia.*

[*The* TOUT *glances in fright in the direction of the voice, and turns to flee.* ANGELA *puts her foot out and trips him. He falls heavily.*

ANGELA. Pretty lady hopes that hurt!

[*The* TOUT *gets up and runs off.*

[COLONEL EDWARD APLIN *emerges from the door of the restaurant. He is a well-dressed, military figure, in the late sixties.*

COLONEL. Forgive my not interfering before; I didn't realize what was happening.

ANGELA. It was most kind; thank you so much.

COLONEL. Are you all right?

ANGELA. Perfectly. In the ordinary way I'd have clonked him on the head; but I have something valuable in my bag, so didn't dare risk a tussle.

COLONEL. It's most unusual for such an incident to take place in Venice—especially in this less fashionable district. I trust it hasn't upset you too much?

ANGELA. No, no. I'm used to looking after myself.

COLONEL. You're travelling alone?

ANGELA [*after a glance at him*]. Yes.

COLONEL. Then—though you're probably in the mood to beware of strange gentlemen—may I offer you something to restore lost energy?

ANGELA. How very kind!

[*He gestures to one of the tables. She sits, and he joins her.*

COLONEL. I suggest a *spécialité* of this place: fresh peach-juice and gin. [*Calling.*] Phillipo!

ANGELA. It sounds a little different from my usual mid-morning cup of tea, but I'd love to try it.

COLONEL. Splendid!

[PHILLIPO, *a young, good-looking, smiling Italian waiter, arrives.*

PHILLIPO. *Colonnello?*

COLONEL. *Dammi due bicchieri; la specialita della casa.*

PHILLIPO. *Subito, Colonnello.*

COLONEL. *Con molto ghiaccio.*

PHILLIPO. *Certamente, Colonnello.* [PHILLIPO *goes off.*

ANGELA. How clever to speak the language.

COLONEL. Not as well as I should considering I live here most of the year.

ANGELA [*looking at him with increased interest*]. How wonderful! Whereabouts?

COLONEL. I have a flat near by—in a palazzo overlooking the Grand Canal.

ANGELA [*even more interested*]. Am I sitting with a millionaire?

COLONEL [*smilingly shaking his head*]. Merely a retired member of his late Majesty's forces living on a colonel's pension.

ANGELA [*a little crestfallen*]. Oh!

COLONEL. But my late father foresaw the Plastic Age, and my pension's augmented by his forethought.

ANGELA [*her eyes gleaming again*]. Ah!

[PHILLIPO *returns with the drinks.*

PHILLIPO. *Ecco, signora.*

COLONEL. *Bene. Grazie.*

ANGELA. Yes; *grazie.* It looks delicious.

PHILLIPO. Is delicious, *signora.* And the second you find even more delicious. [*He goes off.*

ANGELA. Your very good health, Colonel—?

COLONEL. Edward Aplin. And may you have nothing but pleasant experiences in Venice in future, Mrs—?

ANGELA. Angela Fairbourne. I'm sure that I shall—[*gazing at him admiringly*] now.

[*They drink.*

Uuum! I see what he meant about wanting a second.

COLONEL. Shall I order it immediately?

ANGELA. Not unless you wish to sit here till nightfall listening to my very dull life story.

COLONEL. I'm sure it's anything but dull.

ANGELA. A small house in the depths of Wiltshire can't compare with living on the Grand Canal.

COLONEL. It sounds delightful.

ANGELA. Oh, it is. [*A little pathetically.*] But lonely. You see, my husband has—what my beloved daily calls—"gone aloft."

COLONEL [*nodding sympathetically*]. Ah. I understand why you used the word dull.

ANGELA. You mean—?

COLONEL. My wife is also—"aloft."

[*She puts her hand on his arm, and for a moment they sit in silence.*

ANGELA [*musingly*]. Of course it's not the right way to think of it, but I should never have been able to come to Venice if Bertie hadn't—[*she glances upward*]. He always maintained, very vehemently, that it "stank."

COLONEL. So did Margaret. Though everywhere except Bournemouth smelt to Margaret.

ANGELA [*lifting her glass*]. Let's drink to our less sensitive but—happier noses. [*They clink glasses, and drink happily together.*

COLONEL. How long are you staying in Venice, Mrs. Fairbourne?

ANGELA. It rather depends. You see, I've had the most amazing piece of luck.

COLONEL. At the Casino on the Lido?

ANGELA. On the Premium Bonds in London. I've won a thousand pounds.

COLONEL. Impossible!

ANGELA [*excitedly*]. That's what I've always thought. But into the pigeon-hole at my hotel last week there suddenly flew one of those common-looking Income-Tax-like envelopes. And inside it said one of my dear little bonds had won me "one thousand pounds."

COLONEL. How very exciting.

ANGELA [*ruefully*]. Too exciting. It's embroiled me in unbelievable trouble.

COLONEL. How?

ANGELA. Well, I immediately wrote off to my friend Mary Truscott, in London, telling her to collect the money, bring it here, and we'd have a gorgeous spree taking gondolas everywhere and eating scampi every meal.

COLONEL. But surely only you can draw the money?

ANGELA. No; I filled in a form saying I authorized Mary to collect it on my behalf. And enclosed the winning bond to show I really owned it.

COLONEL. Then why the trouble?

ANGELA. Half an hour ago I got this telegram [*she takes it from her bag*]. "IDIOT STOP CANNOT COLLECT FILTHY LUCRE WITHOUT BOND STOP SEND IMMEDIATELY."

COLONEL [*puzzled*]. I thought you had?

ANGELA. So did I! But in all the excitement I somehow hadn't. [*She produces envelope from her bag.*] It's been sitting in my bag all the week masquerading as general rubbish. I was on my way to the post office with it when that man accosted me.

COLONEL. Ah, so that's the valuable object you have in your bag.

ANGELA. Actually I meant this gold cigarette-case of Bertie's [*taking it from her bag*]. It is rather valuable, I believe.

[*She hands it to him.*

COLONEL. Very heavy. It should be. [*He passes it back.*] Isn't it a little unwise to carry it about?

ANGELA [*sadly*]. This is probably the last time I shall. After I've posted my letter I'm going across the square there to the shop of a man with lovely long eyelashes.

COLONEL. You're going to sell it?

ANGELA. I must. You see my friend Molly not having arrived——

COLONEL [*interrupting*]. Molly?

ANGELA [*a little flustered*]. Did I say Molly? How stupid! I meant Mary, of course. [*The excuses tumble over each other.*] Her husband calls her Molly, and I get muddled occasionally. But her name's Mary, of course. As I was saying, Mary not having arrived has put me in an awful fix.

COLONEL. Financially?

ANGELA. Yes. When I heard about my fortune I decided to stay on a bit. So instead of paying the hotel bill, I spent the money celebrating. Now the manager's agitating, and owing to my stupidity it'll be several days before Mary arrives.

COLONEL. You must, of course, allow me to tide you over.

ANGELA. You mean lend me money. [*A little too anxiously.*] That is what you mean, isn't it?

COLONEL. How much did you hope to get for the cigarette-case?

ANGELA [*almost too pat*]. Twenty-five pounds. [*Strongly.*] But I wouldn't dream of borrowing it. Let alone from a stranger— [*beaming at him*] however gallant. I can't think what made me tell you about it. Yes, I can. This deceitfully innocent nectar.

COLONEL. I'm delighted it's potent enough to save a charming innocent from being fleeced. Please allow me to play the gratifying rôle of Saint George.

ANGELA [*wistfully*]. For all you know I may only be "playing" the rôle of the damsel needing saving.

COLONEL. A damsel with a thousand pounds practically in her handbag is no great risk.

ANGELA. Yes, at least I have the proof [*hastily taking the bond out of the envelope*]. Thank goodness that I forgot to post it, now. [*She holds it out to him.*] There it is, you see: Premium Savings Bond K 2026581.

COLONEL [*not taking it*]. I believe without seeing.

ANGELA. No, no; I insist you look.

COLONEL. My dear, however insistent, you can't make me see.

ANGELA [*looking at him in amazement*]. You mean...?

COLONEL [*cheerfully*]. That I wouldn't know if you were holding a blank paper in your hand.

ANGELA. You're blind?

COLONEL. Completely blind.

ANGELA. I can't believe it.

COLONEL. You couldn't delight me more.

ANGELA. But your eyes—they look perfectly normal.

COLONEL. My particular complaint doesn't affect their appearance, merely their usefulness.

ANGELA. You poor, poor man.

COLONEL. Not at all. I remember the beauty of Venice without having to see its ghastly modern "improvements."

ANGELA. I simply can't believe it.

COLONEL. Many years pretending to be a brave and fearless soldier made me good at counterfeiting.

ANGELA. But you saved me from that tout; how, if you couldn't see?

COLONEL. Loss of one sense has improved all the others.

ANGELA [*obviously not satisfied, and moving her head from side to side in front of him*]. Can't you see at all?

COLONEL. Not even the colour of your hat.

ANGELA [*quickly*]. How do you know I'm wearing a hat?

COLONEL [*after only a momentary pause*]. It seems likely that a lady from the cool depths of Wiltshire would wear a hat on a hot morning in Venice.

[*She looks at him unsatisfied and puzzled.* Aren't you wearing a hat?

ANGELA. Yes, I am. [*After a little pause; referring to her coloured close-fitting one.*] A broad-brimmed white straw.

COLONEL [*after a moment*]. I'm sure that it becomes you. [*With almost a mocking smile.*] I only wish I could see you in it.

ANGELA [*ashamed; and impulsively putting her hand on his arm*]. I'm a wicked woman.

COLONEL. Why?

ANGELA. Never mind why; I am.

COLONEL. Then I like the sound of wickedness! And insist on subsidizing it to the extent of twenty-five pounds. [*He takes a repeater-watch from his pocket.*] Now, let me see, what time is it?
     [*He presses the switch; it sounds a quarter to twelve.*]
ANGELA. What a gorgeous watch!
COLONEL. Isn't it? [*Showing it to her.*] Muriel gave it to me when I had the accident.
ANGELA [*sharply*]. Muriel?
COLONEL. My wife.
ANGELA. I thought you said her name was Margaret.
COLONEL [*after only the slightest pause*]. Margaret was my first wife; Muriel my second.
ANGELA [*without conviction*]. Ah, that explains it. [*She examines the watch.*] Gold and enamel; she had excellent taste. How does it work?
COLONEL. You slide this [*demonstrating*], and it chimes the nearest quarter.
ANGELA. It's quite lovely.
COLONEL [*listening to it*]. Quarter to twelve. Correct?
ANGELA [*looking across the square*]. A few minutes after.
COLONEL. Then you've just time to catch your friend with the long eyelashes before he goes to an interminable lunch. Tell him you've changed your mind.
ANGELA. But I can't. I must have the money.
 [*The* COLONEL *takes a wad of Italian banknotes from his pocket; counts out a quantity; feels for her bag, opens it, and puts in the notes.*]
COLONEL. You have the money. Fortunately I'd just been to the bank.
ANGELA. How very kind and generous. You shall have it back immediately Mary arrives—at the week-end at the latest.
COLONEL. Suppose you repay my kindness by bringing her here, and letting me give you both a *spécialité*. Shall we say on Saturday at eleven?
ANGELA. Saturday at eleven it shall be. And [*with her hand on her heart*] *Grazie, grazie*, for everything.
COLONEL [*smiling*]. *Prego!*
 [*She picks up her bag and leaves. Just as she is about to go*

off she turns, and looks back at him curiously. Then, suddenly, she lifts her hand and waves gaily.

[*Though gazing in her direction, the* COLONEL *makes no acknowledgment. She waves again, more energetically. Still no response. She shakes her head in a puzzled way, shrugs happily, and goes off.*

[*The* COLONEL *gazes after her, also with a look of puzzlement. Then, moving his chair to call the waiter, his hand feels the letter that* ANGELA *has left on the table. He picks it up, and ponders. Then, suddenly, he has an idea.*

COLONEL [*calling*]. Phillipo!

PHILLIPO [*appearing almost immediately*]. *Colonnello?*

COLONEL. The lady brought me a note. In case it mentions her, I don't want to ask her to read it. Will you do so?

PHILLIPO. *Certamente, Colonnello.* [*He takes the letter from the envelope.*] *Ecco.* [*Starting to read.*] "My dearest Mary, what a silly billy I am——"

COLONEL. No, stop! That's one of her own letters. Is there nothing else in the envelope?

PHILLIPO [*looking*]. Only a sort of ticket, *Colonnello.*

COLONEL. What does it say?

PHILLIPO [*reading*]. "Premium Savings Bond. Issued by the Lords Commissioners of H.M. Treasury under Section One of the National Loans Act of 1939..."

[*Exactly as* ANGELA *did, the* COLONEL *shakes his head in a puzzled way; then shrugs happily.*

COLONEL. Well, we'll wait and see what happens on Saturday, Phillipo.

[*The lights dim to a complete blackout. Gay Italian music is heard.*

[*When the lights fade up again, the square is bathed in morning sun. The tables are clear.* PHILLIPO *is attending to the geraniums.* ANGELA *hurries on.*

ANGELA. *Buon giorno*, Phillipo.

PHILLIPO. Ah! *Buon giorno*, Signora Fairbourne. How pleasant to see you. But are you not early? *Il colonnello* tell me "eleven o'clock" on Saturday.

ANGELA. I am a little before time. [*With meaning.*] Purposely.
[*She sits at one of the tables.*]

PHILLIPO [*smiling conspiratorially*]. You want secret of peach-juice cocktail, *signora*?

ANGELA. No; I want another secret. [*Watching him.*] In confidence—you understand me?

PHILLIPO [*doubtfully*]. Well, *signora*—

ANGELA [*holding out her gold cigarette-case*]. Have a cigarette?

PHILLIPO. Thank you, *signora*. [*He takes the lot.*]

ANGELA. I see you do understand me. How long have you known the colonel?

PHILLIPO. Oh, long time, *signora*—maybe six year—

ANGELA. As much as that?

PHILLIPO [*gaily*]. Maybe even more.

ANGELA. Was he blind then?

PHILLIPO. Maybe even more blind, *signora*.

ANGELA [*sharply*]. More blind?

PHILLIPO. I mean he was bad at finding way. Many time I help him home. Now, no need.

ANGELA. No. [*With a sharp look at him.*] He gets about remarkably well.

PHILLIPO. Only in little world he know, *signora*. He never go more than his flat, the shops over there, and this *ristorante*.

ANGELA [*acidly*]. Then it couldn't have been him I saw near the Rialto Bridge yesterday?

PHILLIPO. Near the Rialto Bridge! If he was alone, impossible, *signora*.

ANGELA. Whoever it was was alone all right. And moved off remarkably quickly when I called across the canal. [*She watches him.*] Do you know I have a strong idea [*she continues with hardly a break, but in a slightly louder voice*] that if Regent Street had water flowing down it, it might be almost as beautiful.

PHILLIPO [*puzzled*]. Regent Street, *signora*?

[*She nods slightly in the direction of the square.*] Ah, *buon giorno, Colonnello*.

COLONEL [*coming on to terrace*]. *Buon giorno*, Phillipo. And *buon giorno*, my dear Mrs Fairbourne.

ANGELA [*suspiciously*]. You know I'm here?

COLONEL [*delicately sniffing*]. My favourite perfume is Quelquefleurs; I noticed you wearing it the other evening.

ANGELA. Very clever, *Colonnello*.

COLONEL. Merely a perceptive nose, my dear. But it doesn't detect another perfume. Is your friend Molly not with us?

ANGELA [*sweetly correcting*]. Mary. No, my letter was very slow. But I've had a cable; she's joining me to-morrow. [*Miserably.*] If I'm still joinable. [*Dramatically she lays her hand on his.*] Something terrible's happened.

COLONEL. Not so terrible that a gin and peach-juice won't make it better, I'm sure.

ANGELA [*sadly*]. I think I'm more in the mood for coffee—

PHILLIPO. I make it special—with a little something in it. And for you, *Il colonnello*?

COLONEL. Very well.

PHILLIPO [*going*]. I will bring immediate. [*He goes off.*

COLONEL. Now what's this calamity?

ANGELA. I've had my handbag stolen.

COLONEL [*not quite so sympathetically*]. No. Don't say you've lost your gold cigarette-case.

ANGELA. No, fortunately I'd left that in my evening-bag.

COLONEL. So what did you lose?

ANGELA [*mournfully*]. The twenty-five pounds in lire you'd so kindly lent me.

COLONEL [*after a slight pause*]. How very distressing.

ANGELA. Distressing? It's disastrous! I'd promised to pay my hotel bill, and now I can't. They threaten that either I do by noon, or—*prisione*!

COLONEL [*a little bitterly*]. I shall of course lend you more...

ANGELA [*beaming*]. I knew you'd say that. And as it's only till to-morrow I gratefully accept.

COLONEL. I'll go to the bank and cash twenty-five pounds as soon as we've had our coffee.

ANGELA. Well... er... as I've been there another three whole days and entertained rather a lot, I'm afraid—it's quite terrible—that I must ask if you can make it fifty.

COLONEL [*swallowing*]. Fifty it shall be.

ANGELA. Bless you! [*Getting up.*] I'll go and ring the hotel straight away.

COLONEL. If they've waited three days they can wait another half hour. Drink your coffee, which I hear approaching.

[PHILLIPO *brings in the coffee.*]

ANGELA [*sitting again*]. Yes, of course—how silly of me.

PHILLIPO. See if you like, *signora*.

ANGELA [*sipping*]. Huum! It is [*gesturing and dramatically emphasizing every syllable*] mer-vil-i-o-so! Ass-o-lu-ti-men-ti mer-vil-i-o-so!

PHILLIPO [*delighted*]. You speak Italian, *signora*.

ANGELA. To be truthful, almost only those two words. [*Beaming at him.*] But they're all one needs in Venice.

PHILLIPO. How kind, *signora*, how kind. *Grazie, grazie*—

ANGELA. *Prego!*

[*He goes off, beaming.*]

What a nice man!

COLONEL. Yes. You must introduce your friend Mary to him— [*a little acidly*] *if* she comes.

ANGELA. If—?

COLONEL [*smoothly*]. If she comes to this restaurant with you.

ANGELA. We shall give you a meal here to show how much we appreciate your kindness.

COLONEL. Such gratitude is most touching. [*Hardly changing his tone.*] It makes me less apprehensive about asking you to do something for me.

[ANGELA, *about to drink, chokes.*]

Are you all right?

ANGELA. Yes, yes—just a little coffee in the windpipe. [*Her voice squeaks in her anxiety.*] There's something I can do for you?

COLONEL. There just might be. It depends.

ANGELA [*warily*]. On what?

COLONEL. There are some very lovely and amusing paintings by Carpaccio in a church called San Giorgio——

ANGELA [*interrupting excitedly*]. But I know those Carpaccio paintings. He's my favourite artist. They're wonderful. I spent hours looking at them last week.

COLONEL [*calmly smiling*]. I know you did.
ANGELA [*staggered*]. You know?
COLONEL. I was there when you were.
ANGELA. Impossible!
COLONEL. I'd taken an English friend to see the Carpaccios. He described a woman he particularly noticed because of her rapt attention before each picture.
ANGELA. But how could you possibly connect her with me?
COLONEL. I didn't. Till just now. Your [*imitating her*] "Assolutimenti mervilioso" to Phillipo gave you away. You were repeating the phrase in exactly the same way to the custodian who showed you the Carpaccios.
ANGELA. Well! [*She is not at all happy about this explanation.*] What an extraordinary coincidence.
COLONEL [*blandly*]. Venice is a city of happy coincidences.
ANGELA [*worried*]. Oh! But what has this one to do with my—PERHAPS helping you?
COLONEL [*lowering his voice*]. Can anyone overhear us?
ANGELA [*glancing round*]. No.
COLONEL. Treat what I'm going to tell you with the greatest confidence.
ANGELA. Yes?
COLONEL. It's come to my ears—[*a little overdoing it*] people are so kind to the afflicted—that a certain count who lives near the Rialto Bridge has just bought several paintings for resale.
ANGELA [*suspiciously*]. He lives near the Rialto Bridge?
COLONEL. Yes—why?
ANGELA [*worried*]. One of your little Venetian coincidences, that's all. This count's a picture-dealer?
COLONEL. Only in a sense. He's an extremely wealthy man who dabbles in Art as an excuse for not entering the family tanning business.
ANGELA. So isn't a great connoisseur?
COLONEL. Precisely! Though he has wonderful connexions through his family. My informant thinks that one of the pictures —which the count bought from an impoverished *principessa*—is something rather special.

ANGELA. What?

COLONEL [*slowly*]. A Madonna painted by Carpaccio.

ANGELA. By Carpaccio? The one we've just been talking about who painted the pictures in the Church of San Giorgio?

COLONEL. Is there another?

ANGELA. But if it were by him this picture would be worth thousands.

COLONEL. Exactly why I'm thinking of buying it.

ANGELA [*slowly*]. I begin to see.

COLONEL. Then will you use your eyes for me?

ANGELA [*alarmed*]. Me?

COLONEL. Well, it's so easy to deceive the blind.

[ANGELA *starts with guilt, and upsets her cup and saucer.*]

ANGELA. Oh, I'm so sorry.

COLONEL. What is it?

ANGELA. Nothing, nothing—just the cup upset in the saucer slightly. What exactly do you want me to do?

COLONEL. Others may hear of this picture any time, so I must act quickly. But before I enter into negotiations I want confirmation of the subject, the style of painting, and your view of its authenticity.

ANGELA. You couldn't rely on my judgment.

COLONEL. Your intelligent appreciation of the Carpaccios in San Giorgio makes me think I can.

ANGELA [*sharply*]. Why don't you get a proper expert?

COLONEL. Because if it is a Carpaccio he'd then try and buy it. [*Smoothly.*] Of course I don't expect your advice for nothing. I propose to forget about the little loans.

ANGELA [*hoping to sound disdainful*]. With my Premium Bond money they make little difference. I shall go because I'm intrigued.

COLONEL. Good! While you're there perhaps you'll do something else for me?

ANGELA [*warily*]. What?

COLONEL. Take careful note of the other pictures in the room.

ANGELA [*puzzled*]. You're interested in them, too?

COLONEL. The count has a reputation of being crafty. I don't want him to know which painting I'm really after.

ANGELA. You could never get away with pretending to see the pictures.

COLONEL. I could if you'll memorize every detail of their surroundings.

ANGELA. What sort of detail?

COLONEL. Everything from the time one enters the front door till one reaches the room. Its exact shape and furnishings; where the pictures hang; details of their subjects and colourings; where the window is——

ANGELA [*interrupting sharply*]. Why?

COLONEL [*blandly*]. So that I know what light falls on the pictures. Also who else may live in the house, and whether there are any servants. So that if anyone should come into the room I have an idea of their identity.

ANGELA [*bitterly*]. I see I'm going to earn my little loans.

COLONEL [*sweetly*]. If you also draw me a map of the house you will.

ANGELA. How will a map help you if you can't see?

COLONEL. You'll pinprick the lines.

ANGELA [*watches him for a moment*]. If I may say so, it would be worth far stranger and more complicated efforts if the result is a Madonna painted by Carpaccio.

COLONEL. That's true. [*Briskly.*] Well, if we're going to beat the others to the post I'd better start straight away. What's the count's telephone number? [*He takes paper from his pocket.*] All the particulars are written down here.

ANGELA [*taking paper*]. I'll go and ring him, and arrange an appointment.

COLONEL. How are you going to explain knowing about the picture?

ANGELA. I, too, have an inventive brain, Colonel. [*Getting up.*] Knowing Italian telephones I shall probably be ages. Perhaps you'll be so good as to arrange my money in the meantime?

COLONEL. I will. And meet you back here.

ANGELA [*pensively*]. Thinking it over, fifty pounds may run me a little short. As it's only till to-morrow, would you make it seventy-five?

COLONEL [*wryly*]. Seventy-five it shall be.

ANGELA. Thank you SO much. [*Going.*] Order me a *spécialité*, will you? I shall need it. I can't think why, but I feel as if I were about to take part in a train robbery.

[*She goes off. The* COLONEL *calls.*

COLONEL. Phillipo!

PHILLIPO [*appearing*]. *Colonnello?*

COLONEL. I'm going across to the bank. If the *signora* returns before I do, please give her a gin and juice.

PHILLIPO. *Certamente, Colonnello.*

COLONEL. From the little I heard you seemed to be getting along remarkably well with the *signora* when I arrived this morning.

PHILLIPO. The *signora* wanted to know—[*smiling*] certain things, *Colonnello.*

COLONEL. Did she bribe you?

PHILLIPO [*cheerfully*]. Yes, *Colonnello.*

COLONEL. As well as I do?

PHILLIPO. No, *Colonnello.*

COLONEL. So that I should probably approve of the answers you gave.

PHILLIPO [*smiling broadly*]. I think, *Colonnello.*

COLONEL. Good!

[*As he smiles and gets up the lights fade. Music.*
[*When the lights come up again the terrace is seen lit by coloured bulbs, in the lattice work, and discreet table-lamps. The tables are now laid for dinner.*
[*At one of them the* COLONEL, *sipping a drink, is waiting impatiently. He takes out his repeater watch, and listens in annoyance.* ANGELA *hurries on.*

ANGELA. Oh, I am so sorry to be late, Edward, dear. [*She sits at the table.*] But I've had the most terrible afternoon at the airport.

COLONEL. Your friend Mary hasn't arrived?

ANGELA. No. Isn't it awful?

COLONEL. Why not?

ANGELA [*without a blush*]. Fog!

COLONEL. I haven't smelt fog.

ANGELA. Not here. In London. Never mind, she's sent a cable

saying it's clearing, and she'll be here to-morrow, without fail.

COLONEL. "And evermore he said, 'To-morrow.' "

ANGELA [*innocently*]. I beg your pardon?

COLONEL. A quotation by a poet called John Gower.

[*The arrival of* PHILLIPO *with a drink saves her from having to answer.*

PHILLIPO. I see you arrive so I bring usual, *signora*.

ANGELA. How kind. *Grazie*!

PHILLIPO. *Prego*! I will start meal in five minute, *Colonnello*.

COLONEL. Fine.

[PHILLIPO *goes off.*

To save time I've ordered the dinner; I hope you'll approve.

ANGELA. I'm sure I shall; I feel calmer already. A cigarette and I shall be my old self. [*Taking one from her case.*] Will you have one?

COLONEL. I only smoke cigars, thank you.

ANGELA. I often think I'd like to, but I'm too cowardly. People will stare at women cigar-smokers. I do myself.

[*While chattering she has taken out her lighter. She now lights it, and suddenly holds it out in front of the* COLONEL's *face. He draws back sharply.*

COLONEL. What are you doing?

ANGELA [*with exaggerated apology*]. Oh, I'm so sorry. I was thinking you'd taken a cigarette.

COLONEL. But we were discussing my only smoking cigars.

ANGELA. I was thinking of something else. Something a vet once told me about a litter of Pekingese puppies.

COLONEL. I don't quite follow the connexion.

ANGELA [*mischievously*]. You would if you knew his theory.

COLONEL. Then you'd better tell me.

ANGELA [*shaking her head*]. It would lead to a great deal of discussion, and I know you must be longing to hear about the count.

COLONEL. I am.

ANGELA. Then the vet can wait. [*Lowering her voice.*] Well, it's all going to be much easier than you can have hoped. The room where the pictures are is on the ground floor, on the right, five paces inside the front door.

COLONEL. Yes?

ANGELA. It's furnished as a little drawing-room; I've scribbled down where everything is, and will draw you a proper plan.

COLONEL. Splendid.

ANGELA. There are seven pictures; five hanging, and two propped against a sofa. The Carpaccio is about four feet by two and a half, in a gilt frame—rather bashed in the left-hand corner—and hangs so that the bottom of it would be about level with your eyes as you enter the room.

COLONEL. Well done. And your opinion of it?

ANGELA. I just don't know. If I saw it in a gallery, and it was catalogued as Carpaccio, I wouldn't doubt it for a moment. It's exquisitely painted; the Madonna's face glows with ecstasy, and the Child is one of the most glorious babies I've ever seen. It's certainly an Italian sixteenth-century painting, at the latest, and there's no doubt that it could be by Carpaccio. More I can't say.

COLONEL. You've said enough to make me want it.

ANGELA. I knew you would. [*Happily.*] That's why I left a deposit on it.

COLONEL [*aghast*]. You did what?

ANGELA. You know the seventy-five pounds you gave me yesterday.

COLONEL [*apprehensively*]. Yes.

ANGELA. Well, when I went to settle my hotel bill last night I'm blessed if it wasn't full of errors.

COLONEL. So you refused to pay?

ANGELA. Of course! I went out early this morning, and they still hadn't got it right. So I happened to have the whole seventy-five with me when I visited the count.

COLONEL [*ominously*]. Go on.

ANGELA. When I saw the Carpaccio I knew you mustn't miss it. So I paid the seventy-five as a deposit.

COLONEL [*sighing heavily*]. I see. [*Suddenly.*] You didn't give my name?

ANGELA. Of course not. I'm not nearly as silly as you imagine, my dear Colonel Aplin.

COLONEL [*grimly*]. I'm realizing faster and faster that you're the exact opposite, my dear Mrs Fairbourne.   [PHILLIPO *returns.*]

PHILLIPO. I bring mussels now, *Colonnello?*
ANGELA. Mussels! How gorgeous. Yes, quickly.
[PHILLIPO *goes out again.*
ANGELA [*tentatively*]. My bill's sure to be made out correctly when I get back to-night.
COLONEL [*resigned*]. I'll get you another seventy-five in the morning.
ANGELA [*innocently smiling*]. Another hundred and seventy-five.
COLONEL. I beg your pardon?
ANGELA. I've been most dreadfully extravagant. I've seen a shop with the most divine little bit of mink. Only a hundred pounds—ridiculously cheap. I've reserved it; and want to pay and fetch it as soon as the shop opens so that I can surprise Mary in it when I meet her. Can you possibly manage the extra hundred?
COLONEL [*warningly*]. My dear, I know you're being useful to me, but I really——
ANGELA [*interrupting*]. Of course if you'd rather not it doesn't matter in the slightest. It just means I shall have to be busy trying to find some one else kind enough. [*With eyes wide.*] Goodness knows when I shall have time to draw the plan of the count's house.
COLONEL [*with a deep sigh of resignation*]. You shall have the hundred and seventy-five.
ANGELA. You are a dear! Though I was absolutely sure you would be.
COLONEL. Why?
ANGELA. Because of my vet and the Pekingese puppies. You MUST remind me to tell you about it.
[PHILLIPO *comes in with a steaming dish.*
Ah! The mussels. Done with plenty of garlic, I hope?
[*The lights fade. Music.*
[*When the lights come up again it is early morning. The chairs are stacked on the tables, and* PHILLIPO, *in shirt sleeves, is sweeping the terrace.*
[*The* COLONEL, *carrying a light coat and suitcase, hurries in.*
COLONEL. Phillipo!

PHILLIPO. *Colonnello*! [*Guiding him round a bucket to a table.*] Mind the water. But how early you come.

COLONEL. And in a hurry. So sit down with me and pay careful attention.

[*They both sit.*
I have to go to England unexpectedly, I'm catching the ten o'clock plane this morning.

PHILLIPO. Something is wrong, *Colonnello*?

COLONEL. I hope not. Now there are one or two things I want you to do for me [*passing him a pile of lire notes*] if you will.

PHILLIPO. I shall be pleased. [*Counting notes.*] Very pleased.

COLONEL. I haven't let any of my friends know that I'm going; so you'd better not know. Or have seen me this morning.

PHILLIPO. I saw you last yesterday afternoon, *Colonnello*.

COLONEL. Good. In case I may be—delayed, I've packed two bags and left them at the station. Here is the receipt. If I want them I shall write asking you about your two "children."

PHILLIPO. I will then immediately send the bags.

COLONEL. Without advertising the fact. Next: this note. [*Gives it to him.*] It's for Signora Fairbourne. I have an idea she'll come here this morning...

[ANGELA *has in fact entered quietly behind them.*
ANGELA. Your idea is perfectly correct, Edward.

PHILLIPO. *Signora*!

ANGELA. Well, this is a surprise. I got up at dawn to see the fish-market. But what on earth are you doing here so early, Edward?

COLONEL. Leaving you a note, my dear.

ANGELA. Then how fortunate that I returned from the fish this way. [*Firmly sitting.*] It'll be so much nicer to hear its contents than read them.

COLONEL. I only have a short time, but may I offer you breakfast in the shape of a cup of coffee?

ANGELA. How kind.

COLONEL [*to* PHILLIPO]. *Due caffelatte.*

PHILLIPO. It cannot be quick so early, *signora*.

ANGELA [*gaily*]. I'm in no hurry.

[PHILLIPO *smiles at her and goes off.*

Now what's this intriguing note, Edward?

COLONEL. Poor Muriel's had a fit.

ANGELA. I thought poor Muriel was beyond having fits.

COLONEL. You're confusing her with Margaret.

ANGELA. I must be.

COLONEL. Although we're separated, I'm still very fond of Muriel. As we're apparently about to be separated for good, I'm flying to her bedside this morning.

ANGELA. So that's why you're taking the ten o'clock plane.

COLONEL [*surprised*]. You know?

ANGELA [*innocently*]. Another of your strange Venetian coincidences. I went to the booking place—to check when my friend Mary was arriving—and there on the outgoing list was your name.

COLONEL [*acidly*]. Was your friend Mary's name on any incoming list?

ANGELA. Yes, isn't it lovely? She'll be here to-morrow.

COLONEL. I thought she was due this morning?

ANGELA [*beaming*]. Another little delay. [*Distressed.*] I am sorry you're going to miss her.

COLONEL. So am I.

ANGELA. And what terrible news that you've also missed the Carpaccio Madonna.

COLONEL [*after a little pause*]. I—don't quite understand.

ANGELA. Surely you've heard?

COLONEL. What?

ANGELA. That it's been stolen. Apparently the count found it missing when he got back at about two o'clock this morning.

COLONEL. No!

ANGELA. Some one got him out of the way with a false message about having a picture to sell far in the country. Then forced the latch on the window of the very room the Carpaccio was in; and went off with it.

COLONEL. How do you know all this?

ANGELA. It's in the stop press.

COLONEL [*shrugging*]. Oh, well! We must just hope that it wasn't a genuine Carpaccio.

ANGELA [*indignantly*]. I shall be very angry if it isn't after all my trouble.

COLONEL [*slowly*]. I don't quite follow you, my dear.

ANGELA [*smiling sweetly at him*]. Don't you, Edward? Well, let's say that I'm silly enough to have an idea who the—present owner of the Carpaccio is.

COLONEL. In that case you must go to the police, my dear.

ANGELA [*naively*]. They wouldn't help me buy my little bit of mink.

COLONEL. I was under the impression that I'd already done that.

ANGELA [*pensively*]. I really must learn Italian before I come to Venice again; lack of it causes such misunderstanding. When I got back to the fur shop I found it wasn't a hundred pounds the mink cost, but two hundred.

COLONEL [*adamantly*]. No, my dear!

ANGELA [*wide-eyed*]. You won't lend it to me—till Mary arrives?

COLONEL. No!

ANGELA [*cheerfully*]. Oh, I think you'd better, Edward.

COLONEL. Why?

ANGELA. Because a hundred is ridiculously little when one thinks of the price of a Carpaccio.

COLONEL [*politely*]. You seem to suggest that I'm concerned in its loss.

ANGELA [*horrified*]. I'd never dream of suggesting anything so horrid, Edward. [*Ruefully insinuating.*] But there are certain evil-minded people who might possibly think so if they knew how you first got me under a strong obligation by lending me a paltry twenty-five pounds.

COLONEL [*interrupting equally smoothly*]. Plus another seventy-five pounds, together with substantial expenses; followed by a further hundred and seventy-five pounds. Not so paltry when one considers what those same evil-minded people might call the cock-and-bull story that supported your requests for the loans.

ANGELA [*indignantly*]. England's Premium Bonds cock and bull!

COLONEL. There was never any proof that you'd actually won.

ANGELA. But I was most careful to leave the winning bond and my letter to Mary so that you could have them checked.

COLONEL [*so charmingly*]. There was a bond and a letter, certainly. But was it a WINNING bond; and is there such a person as Mary?

ANGELA [*equally charming*]. If you'd any doubts—which is absurd—it might be considered even more probable that the loans were merely to trap me into doing what you wanted.

COLONEL. You have a wonderful imagination, my dear.

ANGELA [*sweetly*]. Haven't I? It's even suggested that our first meeting wasn't as much due to chance as I supposed. That you sat in the Carpaccio church until you saw some one possible. And that you then arranged for a tout to drive her here, where you sat waiting.

COLONEL. How absurd!

ANGELA. Isn't it? As absurd as the idea that you've known for some time about the Madonna, but didn't want to be seen near or at the house, because you might be recognized from previous —exploits. So pretended to be blind. Which attracted confidence and sympathy, and gave a reason for asking some one else to spy out the land.

COLONEL. You think I only pretend to be blind?

ANGELA. Gracious, no. I'm only saying what some people might think. Especially if they knew my vet.

COLONEL. You must tell me about him.

ANGELA. Well, we thought one of the puppies might be blind; I rang the vet, and he told me to light a match just in front of its eyes.

COLONEL. As you lighted your lighter in front of mine?

ANGELA. Did I? In that case all I had to do was watch whether your pupils contracted, and I'd know for certain whether you're blind or not.

COLONEL [*acidly*]. What a pity there's no such simple way of knowing whether Mary and the money exist or not. [*Listening to his watch.*] What I do know, though, is that the friend who's guiding me to the airport is waiting at the corner of the square. Do you see my coat anywhere?

ANGELA. It's on your suitcase here. [*Examining the case with interest.*] Not a very big suitcase. [*With meaning.*] I hope you've got—everything you need in it.

COLONEL. I think so.

ANGELA. I really wouldn't have thought it large enough. Long enough, certainly. [*Puzzled.*] But not wide enough, surely? [*Then happily realizing.*] But, of course. If one [*making rolling-up gesture*] rolls things up they fit wonderfully, don't they? Yes, I'm sure it's large enough after all.

COLONEL. Then perhaps you'll be kind enough to give it to me.

ANGELA [*standing between him and the case*]. You know its odd [*beaming at him innocently*] but I don't feel kind this morning. I don't think I shall give it to you.

[*There is a long silent battle of stares.*

COLONEL [*realizing he's trapped, but still hoping to escape*]. With the cooler weather coming, I'm unhappy about you not having your mink. But I shall miss my plane if I wait to get you a hundred pounds.

ANGELA [*sweetly*]. Maybe you're even more likely to miss it if you don't.

COLONEL [*after a moment's thought*]. Then—for Muriel's sake —I shall let you have most of the money I hoped to arrive in England with. [*He takes out his wallet, and counts out twenty fivers.*] Here you are.

[*He holds them out to her, but, letting them go before she takes them, causes them to fall on the floor. She immediately stoops to pick them up.*

ANGELA. Oh, you've dropped them!

COLONEL. I thought you had them.

[*He steps forward and they collide. She stumbles and there is a slight muddle.*

COLONEL. Oh, I'm so sorry.

ANGELA. It's all right.

COLONEL. I didn't hurt you?

ANGELA. No, no.

COLONEL. You have the money?

ANGELA. Thank you very much. Here is your coat and suitcase.

[*She helps him into his coat.*

COLONEL. Thank you. [*Genuinely.*] I wish I hadn't to go. Very much so. I shall miss your refreshing and enchanting company, Angela, dear.

ANGELA [*touched*]. How very charming. I shall miss you, too, Edward, dear. [*Gazing at him.*] I DO hope those evil-minded people are right about your eyes, and that you CAN see...

COLONEL. I hope they're wrong, and that you have got a friend called Mary who's going to arrive with a thousand pounds.

ANGELA. Probably we shall each know by the next time we meet. For of course we must—even if it's only so that I can repay the loans.

COLONEL. I shall look forward to seeing you for two reasons. You'll find my bank address in the note. In the meantime—good-bye, my dear Angela.

ANGELA. Good-bye, Edward, dear.

[*She puts her hand into his; he kisses it, and then goes off with his suitcase.*
[*She sits at the table watching him with an enigmatical smile.* PHILLIPO *comes in with two cups of coffee.*

PHILLIPO. *Il colonnello* has gone, *signora*?

ANGELA. Yes.

PHILLIPO. How sad.

ANGELA. Yes. It means I shall have to pay for the coffees. Never mind. [*Picking up her bag.*] How many cigarettes to tell me the truth, Phillipo?

PHILLIPO [*smiling broadly*]. Many, many, *signora*.

ANGELA. Then I shan't be able to hear it [*scuffling about in her bag*] as I don't seem to have even one. [*She turns the contents of her bag on to the table.*] That's very odd. I know I had my gold cigarette-case when I came here. [*Suddenly.*] Quickly! Stop the colonel immediately!

PHILLIPO. He is gone, *signora*. But I am sure he would not take it.

ANGELA. Are you? You wouldn't be if you'd seen the little scuffle about the money he managed to arrange.

PHILLIPO. But *Il colonnello* has much money, *signora*.

ANGELA. Yes; I think it was more as a little revenge. [*Thoughtfully.*] The cunning old—— [*Then smiling happily.*] Fortunately two can play at that game.

PHILLIPO. What game, *signora*?

ANGELA [*lowering her voice*]. Well, absolutely in confidence, Phillipo—I benefited from the scuffle, too.

[*She brings the* COLONEL'*s repeater-watch from her pocket, and, smiling seraphically, holds it near her ear, and causes it to ring out the time.*

CURTAIN

The Wall

A Drama in One Act

By Michael Walker

*winner of the "Yorkshire Post" Trophy
at the Bradford Drama Festival*
1963

© *Michael Walker, September* 1963

CHARACTERS

(in the order of their appearance)

1st Soldier
A Woman
2nd Soldier
A Man
A Captain
A Boy
An Old Woman

Scene: *Either side of a wall dividing a city.*
Time: *The present, alas.*

This play is published in acting edition by "New Plays Quarterly," Evans Bros, Montague House, Russell Square, London, W.C.1, to whom applications regarding amateur performances should be addressed.

The Wall

A SOLDIER *in white gaiters and belt enters from* L. *He looks tired and weary with night-sentry duty. He listens at the wall, and then lights a cigarette, furtively.*
A WOMAN *enters behind him.*

WOMAN [*tentatively*]. Hello.
SOLDIER 1 [*whirling round, dropping cigarette*]. Listen, lady—you wanna make a little more noise! You almost got shot there! [*He retrieves his cigarette.*] God Almighty! Look, my hand's shaking now.
WOMAN. It's—it's quiet to-night, isn't it?
SOLDIER 1. Quiet?
WOMAN. No noise.
SOLDIER 1. Oh yeah, yeah, that's right. [*He looks at wall.*] Very quiet.
WOMAN [*flirting*]. And lonely too—lonely for a soldier just standing—
SOLDIER 1. They are there though!
WOMAN [*nervously*]. Who?
SOLDIER 1. I can hear them. They creep around like cats—soft-soled shoes! They stand on the other side here, listening. But I know when they're there.
WOMAN. Are they there now?
  [SOLDIER *puts ear nearer wall. The* WOMAN *comes closer and listens too.*
SOLDIER 1. No. [*He pauses as he sees how close she is.*] Not now.
WOMAN. It's quiet over there, then, too.
SOLDIER 1 [*moving away*]. It isn't always.
WOMAN. No?
SOLDIER 1. Night like this—stars out—quiet—you relax. Then suddenly—a shout, running feet—a shot.

WOMAN [*quickly*]. A shot? [*There is a pause.*
SOLDIER 1. Then it's quiet again. [*Throws cigarette down.*] There's a quiet that's peaceful, lady, and there's a quiet that isn't. This kind of quiet I don't like. No sir!

WOMAN. Perhaps—perhaps imagination has a lot to do with it: a man calls his dog, children scampering past, a late car backfiring.

SOLDIER 1. And the groans? [*Shakes his head.*] Sorry, lady. Some people may like to think that sort of thing—explain it away. But that wall is there. You've just got to look at it and ask yourself—why?

WOMAN. Why? [*Smiles ruefully.*] I used to live on the other side.

SOLDIER 1 [*guardedly*]. Oh? [*Moves away slightly.*] And when was this?

WOMAN. Not long ago. We have a house on the corner opposite here. You can see it. [*Points and moves back.*] You could see it before. Now I can only point. The window of the very room where I was born is just overlooking the wall.

SOLDIER 1 [*lights another cigarette*]. Yeah? Well, you'd better be getting along home. It's late.

WOMAN [*ironically*]. My home?

SOLDIER 1. Sorry—where you live then.

WOMAN. But there's no danger, is there? You said yourself—it's quiet.

SOLDIER 1. Look, if you belong on the other side, what are you doing over here? I suppose it's all right or they wouldn't let you stay. But how come, anyway?

WOMAN. I was shopping. In those days you could. If you had enough money you could buy things they didn't have over there; if not, you could always come across and earn some, or look sorrowful in your relatives' front room. They sometimes gave you something.

SOLDIER 1. So you were shopping?

WOMAN. I was coming back down this road behind us. [*Points.*] I had a parcel in one hand and a second-hand coat for my baby in the other. [*Holds these memories in her hands.*] And when I got here, there wasn't a street any more. They'd started the wall. [*Drops the parcels.*]

SOLDIER 1. Oh. I see.

WOMAN. It wasn't very high then. I stared. What does it all mean, I wondered. What's it for? Then I saw my husband standing on the other side. He had our little boy with him. He saw me looking and he put his hand up, like this. [*Holds an imaginary baby and touches it.*] He pretended to be wiping the baby's nose but his fingers went—[*motions with her hand*]—like that! "Stay where you are—don't come—go back!" I just stared. He stared back at me, and all the time they were putting more and more slabs of concrete on to the wall, and it rose higher. [*She reaches up the wall.*] It was like water rising between us—drowning! [*She stops and bows her head.*] I cried. Before the last stone was fitted I could see he was crying too. And the baby was—frowning, puzzled. [*Shakes her head.*] Just look at it, you say. Just look at it and ask yourself why. [*Sighs.*] I don't know why. My baby—he doesn't know why. Can you tell us?

SOLDIER 1. God, lady, I wish I could.

WOMAN. They fling it up and you stand guard on it. Can you tell me why that is? [*Pause, throws off her worry.*] Could I have one of those cigarettes, please?

SOLDIER 1. Sure.   [*Gives her one and lights it.*

WOMAN [*trying to attract him*]. I'm very grateful.

SOLDIER 1. I wish you hadn't told me all that, lady.

WOMAN. It's the truth. I thought you might like to know.

SOLDIER 1 [*moving away*]. The truth doesn't always help. It's bad enough as it is—walking up and down all night—waiting and listening.

WOMAN. I wait.

SOLDIER 1. You think he might try to come and join you?

WOMAN. I daren't think, soldier. [*Taps cigarette and moves off.*] I just wait without thinking.

> [*He watches her go and, more sadly now, he moves off himself. As he paces slowly away a soldier "on the other side" paces on as if the one were drawing the other. As he comes farther in a tall thin man strolls on. The* SOLDIER *stiffens and then, quickly, he wheels round with a gun pointing.*

SOLDIER 2. Halt! Turn round, you.

MAN. I only wanted——
SOLDIER 2. I said, turn round. Go back.
MAN. Back?
SOLDIER 2. Back there. You're not allowed here.
MAN. I live here.
SOLDIER 2. This is a military position—civilians aren't allowed.
MAN. Your military position is right outside my front door.
SOLDIER 2. You'll be given new quarters soon. Now go back.
MAN. What's your name, soldier?
SOLDIER 2. "Soldier" will do. Never mind my name.
MAN. Don't soldiers have names, then?
SOLDIER 2. What do you want to know it for? If you want to report me my number is enough.
MAN. Men aren't numbers, lad. What did your mother call you?
SOLDIER 2 [*slyly*]. Son.
MAN [*blinking*]. May I call you son?
SOLDIER 2. Get about your business unless you want me to take you in for questioning.
MAN. Have I done something wrong? Just to ask your name?
SOLDIER 2. You're asking for trouble!
MAN. Not trouble—just talk. I'm lonely. Don't you ever get lonely?
SOLDIER 2. Talk is trouble.
MAN. I'm beginning to think it must be. [*Looks at wall.*] On a frontier the language is a barrier, but in a city they have to build a wall.
SOLDIER 2. Look! You'd better shut up!
MAN [*going to wall*]. Each brick, each block of masonry—an unspoken word; each line of mortar—a silent thought. And that barbed-wire on top—[*turns and sees soldier pointing gun*]—that speaks loudest of all.
SOLDIER 2. I warned you!
MAN. Don't you want to talk, son?
SOLDIER 2. It is forbidden!
MAN. But your gun is talking. Can you hear what it says?
SOLDIER 2. Duty!
MAN [*pointing at wall*]. Is that your duty? Have you got barbed wire round your heart too?

SOLDIER 2. I only do what I'm told.
MAN [*nodding*]. Yes, you've been brought up well.
SOLDIER 2 [*sneering*]. Well, you're not a soldier.
MAN. A soldier is only a man in uniform. Does a badge make so much difference?
SOLDIER 2 [*proudly*]. It's a mark of belonging.
MAN [*bitter*]. Like a cross, a swastika—the brand they burn on sheep—the mark of Cain!
SOLDIER 2. You're drunk!
MAN. No. But thirsty. Perhaps you get thirsty too. Do soldiers get thirsty?
SOLDIER 2. Now don't try to be clever. I could take you in, you know.
MAN. You walk up and down all night past my door. Why don't you come in with me? I have some drink, a fire. You'd be very welcome. Just for a few minutes, eh? The door's off the latch. Just slip in, any time. I don't sleep. I'm a sentry too, like you—only I don't know what I'm guarding.
SOLDIER 2. Take a tip from me and guard your tongue! Many of my comrades would have arrested you as soon as you refused to go. You're lucky!
MAN. Lucky to have met a man who won't shoot me? Yes, I think I am. That's what a wall does for you—places new values on little things. Well? Will you come sometimes for a drink and a chat?
SOLDIER 2 [*pause*]. Perhaps!
MAN. Perhaps? [*Smiles.*] When I was a boy my mother said "perhaps" and I was disappointed. Now I am a man and I've waited so long that when a boy says "perhaps" I feel hope. Is not that strange?
SOLDIER 2. You're a strange man. [*Shrugs.*] Look, you're all right, but you'd better go.
MAN. All right, son. But please come, please, if you can at all. You'll make up for so much that's happened. [*He goes.*
SOLDIER 2 [*watching him depart and following him*]. Fool!
  [*On the other side the* 1ST SOLDIER *enters as* SOLDIER 2 *goes off. The* WOMAN, *who has been waiting, steps out of the shadows.*

SOLDIER 1. You still here?

WOMAN [*ingenuously*]. I finished my cigarette.

SOLDIER 1. All right! Here. [*Gives her one and holds match.*] You know—[*smiles*]—you don't want to hang around like this. You're liable to give some one the wrong impression.

WOMAN. How is that? [*She smiles faintly.*

SOLDIER 1 [*youthfully teasing her*]. Oh, come on, lady! A soldier, young and strong, away from home, and a woman walking up and down all night asking him for cigarettes. He might make a very awkward mistake! [*He grins.*

WOMAN [*smiling and moving forward*]. He might not.

[*His grin fades. He is embarrassed and slightly disgusted.* [*Explaining.*] Have you ever stayed with relatives until they were sick of you? Have you ever been told to "get out" by your own kind? [*Shrugs.*] You see, most that come over—once they're here they're quite happy to be "rehabilitated," I think they call it. But because I want to stay—because I have to wait—[*sighs*]—I don't blame them. But on the other hand, I've got to live. [*Tries again.*] I'm not ugly, am I?

SOLDIER 1. You sure are not, but—well—what about this husband?

WOMAN. Because I love him—because of the wall—we have a strange marriage. I'm here, my morals are over there.

SOLDIER 1. Well, I'm sorry but— [*He shakes his head.*

WOMAN. Don't you like me?

SOLDIER 1. It isn't that, lady. [*Moves away.*] But, gee, a married woman! [*Firmly.*] Other guys maybe, but not me.

WOMAN [*annoyed*]. Would you let me starve?

SOLDIER 1 [*kindly*]. I'll give you something. [*Takes out wallet but has second thoughts as he sees her face.*] Say—

[*Puts wallet back.*

WOMAN. You see? Charity demands so much. It's easier for us to work for what we get. That's something you learn very quickly when you need help.

SOLDIER 1. I'm sorry. I didn't mean nothing. Here, let me give you— [*Holds money.*

WOMAN [*angrily*]. Soldier, I'm too proud to take gifts. I take only fees! My husband would rather I sell. Right?

SOLDIER 1 [*embarrassed*]. Well, you see—on duty. And the captain may be round, you know.

WOMAN [*bitterly*]. Is the captain handsome?

[*He looks at her aghast and turns his face away again.*]

SOLDIER 1. Besides, there's nowhere private, you know? I'm sorry.

WOMAN [*seeing him softening*]. I know a place. [*Touches him.*] A safe place. I've used it before, other soldiers——

SOLDIER 1. But I'm supposed to be on guard-duty, lady.

WOMAN [*arms on his shoulder*]. In the middle of the night, who'd know? [*Presses her chin against his chest.*] I'm very good.

SOLDIER 1 [*cocking his ear*]. There's some one coming—better go. [*He moves away.*]

WOMAN [*clinging to his hand*]. You see that old bombed building over there? There's a cellar they haven't demolished yet. I'll wait for you there. Please.

SOLDIER 1. I'm not promising.

WOMAN. I'll wait.

[*She lets go of his hand and separates as the* CAPTAIN *comes on. He watches her slide off quickly. The* SOLDIER *has turned his back.*]

CAPTAIN. Evening, Joe! Everything O.K.?

SOLDIER 1 [*saluting, and hiding cigarette*]. All quiet so far, sir.

CAPTAIN. Well, let's hope it stays that way. Don't want more trouble than we've got already. [*Taking out cigarettes.*] Gotta light? [*He goes forward.*]

SOLDIER 1. Sorry, Captain—I don't carry any matches on duty.

CAPTAIN [*noticing the smoke rising behind* JOE'S *shoulder*]. Listen, Joe. I've been a buck private too, remember?

[*He holds cigarette to his lips and waits.*]

[SOLDIER *produces his cigarette, and* CAPTAIN *lights up. He inhales deeply and walks away rubbing his hands.*]

God, that's better! Well, I'll be glad when I get out of this stinking mess. [*Puffs.*] How's the wife keeping, Joe?

SOLDIER 1. She's fine, but the family—

CAPTAIN. Sick?

SOLDIER 1. No. Growing.

CAPTAIN [*grinning*]. Well, that's life. What the hell d'you get married for if you didn't want kids, eh?

SOLDIER 1 [*also grinning*]. You said yourself you were a buck private once, so do I need to answer that?

CAPTAIN [*slapping his back and chuckling*]. Sure, Sure! Thank God we're all still normal, eh? [*Looks at wall.*] That's one thing to be said for being on the right side of that damned thing. We can all be what we want, eh?

SOLDIER 1 [*looking after the woman*]. You're right there, sir.

CAPTAIN. Yes, sir, I am!   [*Strolls away a little.*]

SOLDIER 1. But you know, sir—I sometimes wonder—

CAPTAIN [*condescendingly*]. What's that, Joe?

SOLDIER 1. Why some of our boys go over.   [*Pause.*]

CAPTAIN [*flatly*]. How's that?

SOLDIER 1. A buddy of mine—[*adds quickly*] well, not a buddy really, but a guy I knew—he went over a couple of months back. Said he was asking for asylum.

CAPTAIN. Damned Reds! Probably got out just in time before we caught up with him. There are always a few like——

SOLDIER 1. But supposing he meant what he said? [*The* CAPTAIN *looks at him.*] Supposing he was going because he liked it?

CAPTAIN. Listen, Joe: that's a load of bull! Who in their right mind would want that kind of set-up? No, either the guy was crazy, or else they had something on him! [*Nods.*] Some just get stuck there by accident—and they're forced to say they want asylum.

SOLDIER 1. I dunno, Cap'n. There might be something in it for some people. They fight damned hard to keep it, don't they?

CAPTAIN. Listen, Joe. Take a bit of advice from me. Any ideas you got like that, you just keep to yourself. O.K.? Don't open your big mouth! You could do yourself a lot of harm.

SOLDIER 1. God, Captain, talk's free, ain't it?

CAPTAIN. Sure, sure. We got liberty and all that—but watch it just the same! You don't want people to think you're a sympathizer with that crowd, do you?

SOLDIER 1. But they're only people, Captain.

CAPTAIN. They're the wrong kind of people, soldier! They're

out to take over the whole damned world. Now, you remember that! What kind of freedom is that anyway—think what we think, or else! [*He turns away and puffs angrily.*

SOLDIER 1. Not much different from "Think what you like so long as you don't say it!" [*He sees* CAPTAIN's *back stiffen. He hesitates. Then meekly.*] Least, that's how it looks, sometimes.
[*He puts out his cigarette. He is afraid.*
[*Pause.*

CAPTAIN [*back to him*]. How long you been on night sentry-go, soldier?

SOLDIER 1. A couple of months, that's all.

CAPTAIN. Yeah? Well, I'll see about having your roster changed.

SOLDIER 1 [*coming nearer, alarmed*]. It's nothing like that, Captain.

CAPTAIN. You got family troubles, you say?

SOLDIER 1. Hell, Captain, not troubles, just little problems. What man hasn't?

CAPTAIN [*turning and staring at him—he tries to feed him an excuse*]. O.K., Joe. I know how it is. Long watch in the night, isn't it? Imagination gets to working overtime, eh?
[*Pause.* SOLDIER *realizes he must agree or else*—

SOLDIER 1. I guess so. Yeah. Maybe that's what it is. Sure.

CAPTAIN [*full of artificial bonhomie now, but with an edge to his voice*]. I knew it all along! You're not the kind that goes sour on us, not the Joe I knew back home! You're one of the good solid guys. [*Slaps his back and turns to go.*] Give my regards to the wife next time you write. I'll see about getting you a spot of leave soon.

SOLDIER 1 [*dismayed*]. Sir, Captain. [*Captain stops.*] I'm up for promotion soon. I've taken the technical papers, so——

CAPTAIN [*facing him*]. You don't say? Well, good for you, boy! That's what I like to see: a man with ambition. Well, when it comes in front of me, I'll do what I can, you know that. You're the kind we need, Joe. We could do with a lot more like you. [*Twists toe on cigarette.*] Reliable! [*The last word cuts like ice. He smiles.*] Well, I've got the rest of the check-points to visit. Better be moving along. [*He notices the* WOMAN *hovering in the shadows.*] Get that civilian out of the way, Joe, eh?

SOLDIER 1 [*sadly*]. Sure, sir.

CAPTAIN [*hesitating as though about to say something*]. Keep your nose clean, boy. [*He goes off.*

[SOLDIER *turns away and slams his fists together. He closes his eyes as the* WOMAN *comes farther in.*

WOMAN. I waited.

SOLDIER 1. That was the captain just now.

WOMAN. He won't come back again, will he? Not to-night?

SOLDIER 1. I guess not.

WOMAN. Then? [*Touches him.*

SOLDIER 1 [*realizing he can do no worse*]. Yeah. Well, you reported a cellar near the wall, see? Maybe it's being used for something illegal, like a tunnel, and I come along just to check up, right?

WOMAN. That's a good idea. [*Takes his arm.*

SOLDIER 1. My name's Joe.

WOMAN. Glad to know you, Joe.

SOLDIER 1. What's your name?

WOMAN. Oh, I'm your girl to-night, soldier. Call me what you want. It doesn't matter.

SOLDIER 1. What's your real name, though?

WOMAN [*pause*]. Eva. [*They go off.*

[*On the other side,* SOLDIER 2 *enters. Behind him a* BOY *bursts on, sees the* SOLDIER, *and hesitates. For some reason he does not go back but turns aside and tries to look nonchalant.* SOLDIER 2 *turns and grabs hold of him, twisting his arm.*

SOLDIER 2. What do you think you're playing at? What's your name? What are you doing here?

BOY [*struggling*]. Let go of me, I've done nothing wrong. Take your hands off me.

SOLDIER 2. As soon as you tell me what you're up to, and if you don't want to talk to me we'll see what the others can get from you.

BOY. I was just taking a walk.

SOLDIER 2. This isn't a park!

[*Pushes him away, and takes out a gun.*

Better tell the truth.

BOY [*fascinated by the gun, and trying to appear airy*]. Oh!—is that a gun? Is it loaded?

SOLDIER 2. Want me to prove it? Loaded or not, it's useful.

[BOY *backs.*

BOY. How old do you have to be to join the army?

SOLDIER 2 [*sneering*]. Old enough to leave your mother, and old enough to shoot the man who's old enough to be your father. [*Looks at him.*] That scares you, doesn't it? Kids like you don't think about killing! We'd soon harden you up in the army though—we've a sergeant who eats children like you.

BOY. Have you ever shot anyone with that?

SOLDIER 2. Why do you ask?

BOY. I just wondered.

SOLDIER 2. Oh, curious, eh? [*Takes hold of him and leads him to wall.*] If you want to know—see that stain? [*The* BOY *looks at stain and recoils.*] It's just a soup stain, lad! I dropped my canteen last week.

BOY [*unconvinced*]. You butcher—you murderer!

SOLDIER 2. You get about your business before I change my mind.

[*He flings him away, and the* BOY *bumps into the* MAN, *who has just entered again.*

MAN. Mind where you're running to, lad! [*Holds him.*] What's all this, then? Has he been getting into trouble?

SOLDIER 2. What are you doing back here? I thought you'd gone home?

MAN. I've been waiting for you.

SOLDIER 2. I didn't promise. Anyway, it was only a few minutes ago.

MAN. Is that all? It seems like hours. Well, well, well. [*Shakes head.*] How about you, sonny? [*The* BOY *is staring across at the stain.*] I don't know what you're doing out at a time like this, but would you like to come home with me and have something to drink? Something hot, soup perhaps, if you don't like beer.

BOY [*"soup" reminding him*]. Here, mister— [*Leads him to stain.*] Does that look like soup to you? That's what he says it is, and nothing more. [*Points.*

D

MAN [*looking*]. It could be soup. That's probably what it is if that's what the soldier says.

BOY. Do you believe what soldiers say?

SOLDIER 2 [*advancing*]. Now just a minute!

MAN [*quickly*]. What about this drink I've invited you to? Aren't either of you going to take me up on it? Good beer, free.

SOLDIER 2. Never mind the beer. I heard what he said. That kind of talk— [*Gun out.*

MAN. That's only youth talking! Where's your sense of humour? You're not going to shoot a lad just for being cheeky? Put your gun down. Put it down—relax. [*Gently turns the gun away.*] What's the world coming to?

SOLDIER 2. It's easy to talk. [*He moves away.*

MAN. Not so very long ago you told me talk was trouble. [*Pause.*

SOLDIER 2. That's your house, you say, over there?

MAN. That's it. You can see I've left the door open. Well?

BOY [*angrily*]. I'm not coming. I don't want to drink with one of them.

MAN [*quickly*]. You'd be drinking with me! Now don't you push your luck too far. [*Smiles falsely.*] Come along now, show the soldier you didn't mean what you said.

BOY. But I did mean every——

MAN [*louder*]. Nothing is ever gained by going into the face of trouble, sonny. Sometimes you've got to retreat in front of a stronger enemy and then— [*Turns and smiles disarmingly at the* SOLDIER, *who peers suspiciously.*] Well, that's better strategy than fighting a war single-handed, isn't it, soldier? [*Nudges him.*] You and me, we could teach youngsters like him a thing or two, eh?

SOLDIER 2. You're not in the army.

MAN. But I was once. Oh, yes, indeed. When you come to my house I've got plenty I could tell you. Let's swap yarns and outboast each other over two mugs of beer, eh?

SOLDIER 2. Well—

MAN. You wouldn't want an impudent little monkey like him to drink it all, would you?

SOLDIER 2. He doesn't know what real drinking is! [*Laughs.*

BOY. Well, you'd know, wouldn't you? I don't want your beer. Let him have it!

MAN. There's enough for all of us. Let's see if we can't all be friends.

SOLDIER 2 [*carefully*]. All right. That's a good idea.

MAN. Of course it's a good idea. Comrades united, eh?

BOY. United in what—murder?

SOLDIER 2. Look! [*Advancing.*] I don't have to take that sort of talk—there'd be no questions asked if I shot you now, on the spot, said you were trying to get over that wall!

BOY. But I thought the wall was to keep spies and agitators out, not us in?

SOLDIER 2. I warned you! [*Hits him.*

MAN [*pushing the* BOY]. Look here, you damned little fool! I don't care who you are or what you say or even if you do get shot... but if it happens now—[*glances uneasily at* SOLDIER]—well, there'd be captains and majors, and police and searchlights, and this poor soldier couldn't come in for a drink with me. Now, isn't all this a bit futile. He didn't build the wall, and he can't pull it down.

BOY [*furious*]. You old fools—you sit back and let it all happen.

MAN. An old fool is better than a young one! [*Hits him, but not hard.*]

SOLDIER 2 [*lifting gun butt*]. He wants teaching a lesson.

MAN [*stepping between them*]. All right. If he cries out you'll have your guard commander down on us. Let him be, eh? Why let him spoil your pleasure?

SOLDIER 2 [*brushing him aside*]. Sometimes this is pleasure—when you can answer clever arguments with a bit of force.

[*Lifts gun.*

MAN [*desperately*]. Tell me—did you ever go to school?

SOLDIER 2 [*glaring*]. Why do you ask?

MAN [*unctuously*]. Well, you're not one of these spoilt namby-pamby university men, are you?

SOLDIER 2 [*lowering gun*]. I was a farmer's son.

MAN. I thought so. Actions speak louder than words.

SOLDIER 2. That's how I feel. [*Walks away a little.*] I think I misjudged you before. I will come with you for that drink.

MAN. Good, good, that's excellent news. We'll have a rare old time, I promise. [*Whispering.*] There are one or two young women live on the first floor so one never knows how this may turn out, eh? [*Nudges him.*]

SOLDIER 2 [*interested*]. Let's go then.

MAN. Oh, but in case they're watching and get—alarmed by the sight of two of us entering together—and also in case some one out here notices, we'd better play it safe, eh?

SOLDIER 2 [*smiling*]. I like you. You're clever.

BOY. He's a pig!

MAN [*impatient at the interruption*]. Little boys should be seen but not heard!

SOLDIER 2. Yes, that's true. [*Goes across.*] Little boys should be seen—[*hits him*]—but not heard.

  [*The* MAN *regrets drawing attention to the* BOY *but smiles when* SOLDIER *turns.*]

All right, comrade. What do you suggest?

MAN. Let's slip in one at a time. Everything's prepared. The door's open, the fire's roaring, and the beer is on the table. As my honoured guest perhaps you would like to go first?

SOLDIER 2 [*suspiciously*]. No. You go first.

MAN. Certainly. [*Starts to go.*] But don't spoil anything, eh?

SOLDIER 2. You don't mind going first?

MAN. Whatever you wish. [*Pause.*]

SOLDIER 2. Very well. I go first. [*Strides off.*]

BOY. You traitor!

MAN. Stay where you are! Look hurt!

BOY. What?

MAN. Look hurt, I said—he's watching.

BOY [*moving past*]. Do you enjoy sucking up to them? Do you enjoy kicking me?

MAN [*elaborately looking the other way*]. Believe me, I don't, but it's only a small price to pay. You wait.

BOY. Wait for what? Till you're both drunk? Celebrating together? You want to come out here and pour your champagne on that stain?

MAN. I know what kind of stain it is. [*Sadly.*] I live across the street, don't I?

BOY. And you make friends with them? [*Walking past.*]

MAN. Stay here! Don't make a sound! If anyone comes on the other side don't answer them! You mustn't attract attention.

BOY [*guardedly*]. Why should I answer back?

MAN. I've seen you before—other nights. I've heard you. [*Pause.*] It's your mother, isn't it?

BOY [*softly*]. My grandmother. She brought me up when my dad was killed.

MAN. Well, just for this once don't answer her.

BOY. Not answer her? I'm all she's got, she's all I've got. No meetings—no letters—just a few words over the wall on certain nights.

MAN. This once, just this once, pretend you aren't there. I promise you'll not be sorry.

[*Pause.* BOY *understands.*]

BOY. What are you going to do?

MAN. Wait and see. [*Pretends to kick him.*] Wait here! [*Louder.*] It's time kids like you were taught a lesson, but don't you worry. One of these days— [*Whispers.*] One of these nights—

BOY [*gleeful*]. You mean?

MAN [*silencing him*]. Pig! [*He goes.*]

[*The* BOY *sinks down beneath the wall, and prepares to wait. On the other side the* SOLDIER I *comes back on angrily, followed by the* WOMAN, *urgent and appealing. Behind them an* OLD WOMAN *shuffles on.*]

WOMAN. Please, soldier.

SOLDIER I. What are you trying to do, lady? Do you want to get me court-martialled?

WOMAN. I had to get you to come with me. I wanted you to see for yourself.

SOLDIER I. Sure, sure, now I've seen. O.K.—good work, girl. Now, good-bye!

WOMAN. It's only a tunnel.

SOLDIER I. So go and dig it. I want nothing to do with it.

WOMAN. But you saw the big stone.

SOLDIER I. Yeah, a beauty, ain't it? I wish you luck!

WOMAN. I daren't ask anyone else, you don't know who you

can trust. They may be informers, and there's only two of us. Look at her. We can't move it.

SOLDIER 1. Then leave it where it is!

OLD WOMAN. It's the last wall, the last wall between us and a cellar on the other side.

WOMAN. Do you know how many hours we've worked trying to find a way through the old cellars? How many nights without sleep? How many brown-paper parcels of earth we've crawled out with?

OLD WOMAN [*holding hands out*]. Look! Look!

WOMAN. Yes, look at her hands. [*Holds her wrists forward.*] That shows how much we've struggled, doesn't it?

SOLDIER 1 [*looking at the deformed fingers and wincing. He lets the hand drop*]. You should get that seen to.

OLD WOMAN. Afterwards—when it's safe.

WOMAN [*following him*]. We wouldn't ask for help if we could do it ourselves. It's just this one stone.

SOLDIER 1. I'm sorry.

OLD WOMAN [*coming to* WOMAN'*s side*]. It wouldn't take you long. Please—?

SOLDIER 1 [*facing them*]. And suppose they found out? Suppose they ask, "Who moved the stone?" [*The two women stare and turn slowly away.*] I'd like to help you; well, God, I'm sorry for you—but I'm a member of the armed forces, and this is mixed up with politics. Supposing they found out, over there, that a soldier had helped with a tunnel? Boom! An international incident. Maybe even— [*Pause.*] You see what you're asking?

OLD WOMAN. Do you see what we're asking?

[*Stands by the wall.*

WOMAN. So. [*Sneers.*] The brave soldier has no courage.

SOLDIER 1 [*incensed*]. Listen—you've no room to sneer! What kind of a game are you playing, anyway? You lure a man away from his post by pretending you're a—pro. And then you expect him to get down on his hands and knees, forget what he's come for, and start doing demolition work! [*Laughs bitterly.*] Did you honestly think it would work?

WOMAN. I've tried eight times with eight different soldiers. [*A half sob.*] I have no money. I daren't ask a civilian. There are people going round saying oh yes, they too want to get relatives over, but if you tell them your plans— [*Shakes head.*] I don't expect it will work, but I have to pray that it will. What else is there?

OLD WOMAN [*hissing at wall*]. Hello? It's me, Hans. Are you there?

SOLDIER 1. What the hell is she doing now? [*He crosses.*

WOMAN [*barring his way*]. They built the wall so no one could cross it. You wouldn't stop us talking over it? You're not as bad as them?

SOLDIER 1. Lady, this isn't a problem for me. Your own police had better deal with this.

[*He turns to leave, but the* WOMAN *crosses and bars his way again.*

WOMAN. Have you no children?

OLD WOMAN. Hans? Are you there, Hans? Hello?

WOMAN. Don't you understand how it is?

SOLDIER 1. I'm not here to understand. I'm not paid to think. [*Takes out whistle.*] They gave me this and a gun. For some situations I use the one; for some situations I use the other. I wouldn't shoot her, lady, but I gotta call the police.

[*Lifts whistle.*

WOMAN. Do you want to kill her?

SOLDIER 1. Aw, for heaven's sake!

WOMAN. She only lives for her grandson. She's not like you and me—young, with our whole lives ahead of us. A little whisper at night is all she has. Take that away and she has—nothing.

SOLDIER 1. I've got instructions.

WOMAN. Have you got compassion? What is she doing, anyway? She's not starting a war, she's not committing a crime. Look at her, for God's sake, is that so terrible?

OLD WOMAN [*urgently*]. Hans, are you there? It's me, son. Can you hear me? Why don't you answer?

BOY [*on other side*]. I— [*Shoves his fist in his mouth.*

SOLDIER 1. There's no one there.

OLD WOMAN. Sssh! I heard something. [*They listen. Silence.*

WOMAN. No. Perhaps he's late.

OLD WOMAN. It's time. He's never missed before.

WOMAN. Leave it a while. You don't want them to hear you. Wait a few more minutes. [*Looks bitterly at* SOLDIER.] Satisfied?

SOLDIER 1. Look lady [*grins helplessly*], I'm just an ordinary guy.

WOMAN. And we're ordinary people. We couldn't move the stone down there, are you afraid we're going to drag down the wall?

SOLDIER 1. I'm sorry, but you gotta try and understand my position.

WOMAN. Have you tried to understand ours?

SOLDIER 1. Lady, I daren't!

OLD WOMAN. Something must have happened to him. He wouldn't miss coming unless something had happened.

WOMAN. Now don't worry. He'll come yet, you'll see. There's plenty of time before dawn.

OLD WOMAN [*aghast*]. But if he hasn't come by then—oh, what shall I do?

WOMAN. We'll think of something, but don't worry, he'll come.

OLD WOMAN [*to* SOLDIER]. Why did they build the wall? Why won't you help with the stone? Why won't anyone do anything for us?

SOLDIER 1. Look, grandma——

OLD WOMAN. Oh, don't talk kind, don't look kind. You're not kind. You're as bad as they are. You're all the same. Nobody's interested, nobody cares, not until it happens to them.

SOLDIER 1 [*sorrowful*]. Don't talk that way.

WOMAN. Why not? It's true. Do you care?

SOLDIER 1. Of course I bloody well care, but I don't want to get involved!

WOMAN. The moment you ignore us you're involved! You're involved far more deeply than if you helped. By doing nothing you're helping them.

OLD WOMAN [*running along the wall*]. Hans? Hans? Are you there? Hans, darling—Hans, it's Gran. Why don't you answer me?

SOLDIER 1. Oh, for God's sake keep her quiet! If she shouts much louder my captain will raise all hell if he finds out.

WOMAN. And their soldiers will raise all hell if they find out. You're here, they're over there, and where are we, soldier? Where are we ordinary people who've done nothing wrong? [*Looks at top of wall.*] We are stretched out up there, hooked on that barbed wire. We can't join you—our loved ones can't join them. We all stay at the foot of the wall, waiting. There's two armies, Joe, but humanity is in between.

OLD WOMAN. I can hear something.

SOLDIER 1. What?

OLD WOMAN. I don't know what, but something. [*Tearfully.*] Hans?

BOY. I'm— [*Stifles himself again.*

OLD WOMAN. Hans! I heard him! Hans, are you there? I know you're there! I heard something—

WOMAN. Are you sure? It could have been their guards talking.

OLD WOMAN. I know the difference! He's over there—something's happened. He might be ill, hurt. God, he might be— [*Almost hysterical.*] Can't you get a ladder, a box, something? Can't you have a look?

SOLDIER 1. No. They'd shoot on sight.

OLD WOMAN. I don't care. Let them shoot. I must see. It's my grandson out there, it's my boy. Please! [*Turns.*] Hans?

BOY [*hissing*]. Shhr! Gran, oh sssh!

OLD WOMAN. I heard him!

SOLDIER 2 [*off*]. What in hell's going on out there?

MAN [*off*]. It's only that kid—take no notice.

OLD WOMAN. Listen—shouting— Oh—they've caught him!

BOY. No, they haven't, Gran. I'm all right.

OLD WOMAN [*enormous relief*]. He's all right!

WOMAN. Come away, you're talking too loud.

OLD WOMAN. Did you hear? Did you hear?

SOLDIER 1. Can't you take her away now before she does any more damage?

OLD WOMAN [*simply*]. What damage have I done?

WOMAN. Yes. Can you answer that?

SOLDIER 2 [*off*]. I'll have to go and shut him up or else my captain will——

MAN [*off*]. No, don't you bother yourself. I'll go and handle this. If people see you go they always think the worst. You stay here, have another drink, I won't be a minute.

SOLDIER 1. There's a commotion on the other side. I think I shall have to call——

WOMAN. And spoil it all? They'll find out about the tunnel. We'd have to start all over again.

OLD WOMAN. But he's there! My grandson is there! I'm here, Hans, I'm here. Are you all right, boy? Is everything all right?

BOY. Yes, Gran. Go away now! Please go away. I'll come again later.

OLD WOMAN. What's the matter, Hans? Are you in trouble? Is some one coming?

BOY. Yes—they can hear you shouting. Now please.

MAN [*striding on*]. What's the matter, you imbecile? Didn't I tell you to keep silent? Do you want to ruin everything?

BOY. It's my grandmother on the other side—

MAN. Come away, then, for God's sake leave before——

SOLDIER 2 [*off*]. Hurry up, damn you! Do you want me to come out there and show you how to deal with that rabble?

MAN. It's all right, comrade! I don't think he'll make any more noise. [*To* BOY.] Just give me time to get him drunk, eh. That's all?

BOY. You mean you are going to have a try at that?

[*Looks at wall.*

MAN. Can you stay quiet?

BOY. I'll try.

OLD WOMAN. Hans, are you still there?

BOY. But what about her?

MAN. Can't you tell her to go away?

BOY. She won't go!

MAN. Please, God, we shall have to risk it anyway.

SOLDIER 2 [*off*]. There's something funny going on.

MAN. I don't want to kill him. I don't want to be like them.

[*Bows head.*

SOLDIER 2 [*nearer*]. What are you up to out there, eh?

MAN. I don't want to—   [*Shakes his head.*

SOLDIER 1. I'm sorry, ma'am, I'll have to get help. I'm not in a position to make this sort of decision, you know.

WOMAN [*desperately*]. Please, please, don't, wait, give us a chance.

SOLDIER 1. I'm sorry. [*He goes.*

WOMAN [*to* OLD WOMAN]. Come away, dear—quick, quick! Come away!

OLD WOMAN. But there's some one on the other side. They're doing something to my boy.

WOMAN. No, they're not.

OLD WOMAN. But they are, I tell you! I know.

SOLDIER 2 [*coming in*]. Now then, what's all this carrying on? [*Pauses and grins.*] Ah, ah! [*Comes in.*] So, you thought you could take me in with a couple of free drinks, eh? You ought to have had more sense, comrade.

MAN. You're wrong, soldier. It's just this boy. I think he's hurt.

SOLDIER 2. He doesn't look hurt. But here, let me show you— [*lifts gun*]—I'll hurt him, and then you'll know how to stop his noise in future.

MAN [*taking knife out, behind* SOLDIER]. Please, don't make me——

SOLDIER 2. Watch this now.

MAN. Soldier, soldier—[*stabs him.*] Oh soldier!

[SOLDIER 2 *gasps, moans, and fumbles a whistle out of his pocket, and gives one loud blast as he falls.*

OLD WOMAN. Hans! Hans! Oh my God! [*Tears at the wall.*] H-a-n-s!

WOMAN. Granny, come away. It isn't Hans. He's gone. Hans has gone.

BOY [*aghast*]. Have you killed him?

MAN. I hope not. [*Distant whistles answering.*] Quick! There's some folding steps in my front porch. I've had them ready for so long. [*Starts off.*] Come on! This is our last chance.

[*They both run off.*
[*Whistles, dogs barking, distant cries.*

WOMAN. I'm going to leave you. I shall have to leave you!

OLD WOMAN. Leave me, leave me! I don't care. I'm not going without my boy.

WOMAN. If they discover the tunnel, we've lost our only chance.

OLD WOMAN. He might be lying there, lying on the ground

above the tunnel. Do you think I want to crawl under the soil now?

WOMAN. Please, please—be reasonable. There's more than just your case at stake. There's mine too. Think of me.

OLD WOMAN. I can't. I can't. Go away and think about yourself. Leave me alone.

[MAN *and* BOY *walk off.* SOLDIER 2 *moves slightly.*

BOY [*off*]. The guards are coming. They did hear his whistle.

MAN [*off*]. There's still time.

BOY [*off*]. No, better run for it. Leave it now. There'll be another chance.

MAN [*off*]. I've waited too long. You run if you want to. I'm not.

BOY [*off*]. You're not—taking the child?

MAN [*off*]. Do you think I'd leave him? Bring those steps for me.

BOY [*off*]. I can't; they're stuck!

MAN [*entering*]. Leave them where they are then. Come on, lad, there's not much time.

[*The whistles and dogs and shouts grow louder all the time.*

OLD WOMAN [*desperately*]. Listen, listen!

WOMAN. It's the guards on the other side. Oh, quick, quick!

[*Pulls her.*

OLD WOMAN. Leave me alone—you've no right——

WOMAN. Don't be stupid!

OLD WOMAN. I want to be stupid! I want to be happy and stupid! Why don't you leave me alone?

BOY [*entering, and running to wall*]. Gran! I'm coming—I'm coming over.

MAN [*holding wrapped baby*]. We can't both go!

[*Pause.*

BOY. What?

MAN. One of us will have to help the other up.

[*They stare at each other. Louder shouts off.*

OLD WOMAN [*running along base of wall*]. Where, Hans? Hans, where are you? Oh, come on, son—come along, love—where are you? Jump, jump! Show me where you are. [*Turns to* WOMAN.] Help me.

WOMAN [*agonizedly*]. How?

MAN. Take the child.

BOY. What?
MAN. Take it. You couldn't support me. I'll bend down, cup my hands. Climb up, hand the child over, and then get over yourself.
BOY. And leave you?
MAN. I'll be all right.
BOY. I can't leave you.
MAN. I'll be all right! If we stand here arguing neither of us will get over and everything will be wasted. Now come on! It's your only chance.
OLD WOMAN. Hans? Where are you? He's there—he's coming —hurry, hurry.
WOMAN. Can you hear us, over there?
MAN. We hear.
WOMAN [*unsure*]. John? John?
BOY. She knows you?
MAN. Eva! [*Pause.*] Eva!

[*The sounds are much nearer. The guards are only a street away.*

Come on, boy—up you get. [*Holds his hands.*] No arguing. Climb up. Mind the baby. [BOY *mounts.*
OLD WOMAN. Hurry, oh, hurry!
WOMAN. For God's sake John—hurry!
BOY. I can manage.
MAN. Quickly!
SOLDIER 2 [*rising on his elbows*]. Traitors! [*Reaches for gun.*
MAN [*unable to move*]. Soldier—comrade—think! Brother— please think.
BOY [*looking over wall*]. Gran!
OLD WOMAN. Oh, Hans! [*The* SOLDIER *shoots.*
Ahhhh! No, no! Come on—come on!
WOMAN. You can make it—come on!
BOY [*choking*]. Catch! [*Drops baby into her arms.*
OLD WOMAN. Hans!
BOY [*weakly*]. Gran, oh Gran— [*He slides down to floor, dead.*
SOLDIER 1 [*rushing in*]. Clear out now, all of you. Shooting! What the hell was it? Any of you hurt?
MAN. Oh soldier! Oh soldier! [*Picks up* SOLDIER's *gun easily.*

SOLDIER 2. Traitors—swine!
MAN [*pointing gun then lowers it*]. I will not become like you.
> [*He drops gun, and* SOLDIER 2 *crawls away. The* MAN *stands facing wall opposite his wife.* OLD WOMAN *weeps opposite the body of her grandson.* SOLDIER 1 *stands silent.*

SOLDIER 1 [*going to* OLD WOMAN]. Come on, Gran, now. It's no use staying here.
WOMAN. Leave—her—alone!
SOLDIER 1. That bloody wall! [*Bows head.*
WOMAN. No. It's not just the wall. It's a long, long gravestone. Do you see it, soldier? It doesn't say "Rest in peace" but "Here peace died." You don't have peace just because you don't have war. As long as there are two sides, peace is on neither.
SOLDIER 1. Lady—I'm sorry.
WOMAN [*vehemently*]. The whole world is sorry! Write that on the wall!
> [*He goes. For a moment she stares at the wall, the child in her arms. The whistles, dogs, sirens, and shouts rise to an unbearable pitch. It is like a long, loud scream—the whole world is full of screaming.*

The CURTAIN *falls.*

After Rome

By Helena Jones

This play owes a great deal to the generous advice and encouragement of Hugh Miller, including first-hand information about the country, ideas about the setting, and suggestions for some of the episodes, very notably the conclusion. It was first performed by the Penzance Young Playgoers on October 29, 1964.

© *Samuel French Ltd* 1964

CHARACTERS

(in the order of their appearance)

ATAULF
CARL } *Barbarians from Northern Europe*
ODO
WANDA, *Ataulf's girl*
VARRO, *a Roman domiciled in North Africa*
FABIA, *his sister, a widow*

SCENE: *A Roman villa in North Africa.*
TIME: *Fifth century* A.D.

Applications regarding amateur performances of this play should be addressed to Messrs Samuel French, Ltd, 26 Southampton Street, Strand, London, W.C.2, or Samuel French Inc., 25 West 45th Street, New York.

After Rome

SCENE: *A Roman villa in North Africa, fifth century* A.D. *The villa is in ruins after a Barbarian raid. The buildings are of red sandstone, and there is green terraced country in the background.* L.: *steps and pillars denoting a building of importance.* D.L.: *an exit to an unseen fountain.* L. *back, another exit. Back: the ruins of a wall. Back* R.: *the ruins of a chapel, from which some of the window-framing has gone.* R.: *steps and pillars of a lesser building, perhaps a bath-house.* R. *back: an exit. The impression is of bright sunlight, mocking the desolation.*

The curtain rises to the sound of shouting. A man is sprawling asleep down R.C. *He is* CARL, *middle-aged for those days; a mean type with a meaningless laugh, a habit of coming too close when speaking, and a way of harping on the same subject. He is going grey, and has a small scruffy beard. He wears a tunic, with a knife in his belt; leg-coverings with criss-cross gartering. There is a round shield near him. He is a killer.*

A second man is prowling around, and it is he who is shouting. He is ATAULF, *a hearty bearded fellow in the prime of life. He is dressed similarly to* CARL, *and carries his shield. He gives the impression of strength, and he, too, is a killer.*

ATAULF [*shouting*]. Carl! Odo! Where the devil you got to, you lot? [*Speaking, weary.*] It's so stinking hot. How the Romans put up with this African sun... [*Shouting.*] Carl! Odo! You all gone deaf? You gone off and left me? Carl...! [*Sees* CARL.] Well I'm damned, look at that! [*Prods with his foot.*] Hey, you, Carl, get up!

CARL [*hand on knife, reaching for shield*]. Eh? You keep off. You'll feel my knife... Oh, you, Ataulf. Let's leave this place. Gives me the shivers. All these ruins. Bad place.

ATAULF. We sweat our guts out looking for food and you go to sleep, you bastard.

CARL. Wasn't asleep. Wrong place, Ataulf. You said there'd be food. No food. You said a good place. Bad place. Nothing to eat. Belly flapping against my backbone. You said...

ATAULF. I know what I said. I said I'm sick of trailing around. I said this country's too hot for Northerners to trail around in. I said let's go back to that villa place with the carved-out buildings in the red cliffs. And you said yes, let's. Damn the flies!

CARL. That place. Not this place. No food here. Wrong place.

[*Tempers are rising.* ODO *has come in. He is a beardless, cocky youth, dressed like the others but with bare legs and home-made foot coverings. His mood varies from febrile high spirits to hungry despondency.*]

ATAULF. Here's Odo. Found the food?

CARL. 'Course not. Wrong place.

ODO [*helpfully*]. Carl thinks it's the wrong place.

ATAULF [*exasperated*]. Oh, it's the wrong place? I'm a fool. Listen, I liked this villa when we raided it. All these shelter places to live in. Terraces of vines and olives. I'm staying. I'm a Northerner. I've done with travelling in this hot South. I'm settling, see? If food's short we'll grow more.

CARL [*affronted*]. Grow food? Us? *I* never came here to grow food. I'm going somewhere else. You staying, Odo? You going to grow food like he tells you?

ODO [*urgent*]. My guts ache. I want food *now*!

ATAULF. We'll find it. Romans store up food. Like our girl tries to. Where *is* that girl? Wanda! We took them by surprise. We slit their throats. They didn't have time for supper... There'll be food here....

[WANDA *has come in. She is a Mediterranean girl, young, scruffy, devoted to* ATAULF, *resenting the others. She wears a rough dress to her ankles, home-made footcoverings, hair dark and loose. She is carrying something behind her back.*]

ATAULF [*sarcastic*]. Oh, *you've* come at last! I've been yelling for you. Where's that food? Women ought to know where women keep things.

WANDA [*apologetic*]. I don't know, Ataulf. I've never lived in houses. I don't know where women keep food in houses.

ATAULF. Well, don't whine about it. I hate whining women. Got anything hidden? [WANDA *shakes her head.* Don't lie to me! Come on! [*He grabs her.* What have you got hidden? You sometimes have...

[*He feels her body, drags her hands round.*
[*She is holding a few sprigs of green leaves.*

WANDA. I've nothing, Ataulf. I picked these... [*Suddenly vivacious.*] I've been looking round. It's so pretty here. All these pillars, and terraces like in Spain. It will be lovely living here.

CARL. Hark at her! "It's so pretty here." So she has a look around while we starve.

ATAULF [*bullying*]. Listen, you girl. You're here to make things comfortable for us men, not to look around. You find food. That's your job. If you can't I'll throw you out.

[WANDA, *crushed, slinks off* R.

CARL. No good, that girl. What did we bring that girl for?

ATAULF. No good any of you. Fool, that's my other name. Clutter myself up with a misery of a girl and two louts who won't grow food...

CARL [*close to him*]. Don't get nasty, Ataulf. We said shares, didn't we? We said we'd stick together. We never said nothing about growing food... ought to have taken prisoners to grow food, instead of killing them all off.. You're not chief, you know —you're only one of us....

ATAULF. 'Course I'm chief. You'd not have had the guts to come back here without me.

ODO [*mutters*]. Nothing here when we got here.

ATAULF [*rounding on him*]. What did you say? Say that again.

CARL [*one-track mind*]. We'll go somewhere else, I'm thinking. Leave that girl behind. She's no good. That's what we'll do.

ATAULF. *You're* thinking? Whose girl is she?

[ODO *is now at top of steps* L., *looking out over the land.*

CARL. You said shares.

ATAULF. Not the girl. She's my girl.... You bastard, Carl, you're no use for anything but fighting, and not much good for that....

CARL [*squaring up*]. Here, no one talks to me like that. Come on, I'll show you if I can fight....

ODO [*delighted*]. Here, you two going to fight?

[*With a joyous yell he hurls himself down the steps, and falls over. No one helps him. The others roar with laughter. He picks himself up. The tension is relaxed. He picks up the thing which tripped him. It is some broken window-framing from the chapel. He shakes it peevishly.*

Curse this thing! Tripped me up. What's it for?

ATAULF [*considering*]. Bit of window? Or just something meant to be pretty? Like all those statues?

[ODO *disgustedly throws it* D.R., *where it lies in the foreground.*

CARL. "All those statues." Waste of time. Not enough to do, these Romans.

ODO [*conversational, crisis temporarily over*]. There's bathhouses here, too. Used to wash. All the time. A fellow told me those Romans had parties while they washed themselves.... You said they grew things. Couldn't have grown much if they was always washing themselves.

CARL. What's the good of washing? Only get sweaty again. Last time *I* had a bath was when I fell in that river in Spain.

[*The others guffaw.*

ATAULF. And I bet you didn't have a party....

ODO. Wish I'd seen that. Old Carl having a bath he didn't want...

[*They savour the joke, slapping each other's backs. The quarrel is forgotten for the moment.*

ATAULF [*change of mood*]. Hell, I'm sleepy. You two keep a look out while I sleep.

ODO. We're not your servants....

ATAULF. Eh?

ODO. I said I was sleepy too.

ATAULF. Some one goes on watch. Got to. Don't want *our* throats cut while we sleep. Wanda!

CARL. Come on, Odo, Another little walk. Some more pretty statues. If we find food we'll have first pick.... [*They go out,* R.

ATAULF [*shouting after them*]. You come right back here with the food! Wanda!

[WANDA *comes in.*

You stay by me while I rest.

WANDA. Yes, Ataulf.

ATAULF. I saw two scorpions this morning.... Nasty things. They can kill. You keep your eyes open. You wake me if you see one. Don't try to kill them yourself.... You listening?

WANDA. Yes, Ataulf.

ATAULF. Not tired again? [*Unsympathetic.*] No energy, you southern girls.

WANDA. Are northern girls all that better than what I am?

ATAULF. You're not tough enough.... You're not bad, though. Not bad at all ... Is there any shade in this place?

WANDA. Over by these pillars.

[ATAULF *moves up* L. *and sits on steps, preparatory to lying down.*

ATAULF. Oh, this stinking heat, and flies too. Why did Romans live in Africa? Romans, weren't they? [*Yawns.*] What are you hanging around for? Sit down and stop fidgetting.

WANDA. You said I wasn't bad.

[*Sits down and leans against him.*

Do you love me, Ataulf?

ATAULF. Oh, shut up. [*Pushes her away, then pulls her back and kisses her, roughly.*] It's too hot. Watch out for those scorpions....

[*He drops back, head out of sight.* WANDA *sits by him, hands round knees. She looks up, sees a bird, raises an arm, whistles.*

WANDA. Ataulf, there's a bird. There aren't many birds.... Hullo, bird. Look, Ataulf, a yellow bird ... You lucky bird, you can live on flies. We can't. They eat us. [*Swats a fly on her arm.*] Ataulf. Look at the bird.... Oh, you're asleep.

[*She stops talking. Presently she hears steps and moves behind the pillar.* VARRO *comes in from* D.L. *entrance. He is a Roman gentleman, sensitive, dignified, without the martial bearing associated with Rome's palmy days. He wears traditional Roman dress, and his hair is round his face almost like a cap. One arm, badly injured, is in a sling. He is not effeminate; the contrast with the barbarians is one of culture. With him is his sister* FABIA, *a youngish matron. She is desperately unhappy.* VARRO *moves across to* D.R. FABIA *wanders about. Her first remarks are distracted and unconnected with his.*]

VARRO. Come and sit here with me, Fabia.

FABIA [*in a dead voice*]. They haven't left anything whole, have they?

VARRO. It's four weeks ago now.... Come and sit with me, dear.

FABIA. Varro, they've broken the chapel. They call themselves Christians, and they've broken the chapel.

[VARRO *goes to her and leads her forward with his good arm.*]

VARRO. We've got to be practical. We must make our plans.

FABIA [*still in a dead voice*]. What do you want me to do?

VARRO. Leave the villa. My dear, we must look for other Romans, survivors of the raids ...

[FABIA *sits down with him,* D.R. *She continues to speak in a drained, desolate manner.*]

FABIA. I don't want to go away. I want to stay with the memories of my life ... all that's left.

[*She picks up, absently, the piece of window-frame which tripped up* ODO, *looks at it, and puts it down in the course of the next speeches.*]

VARRO. My dear sister, it's not possible. If anyone escaped he hasn't come back. There's no one here but you and me. What could we do if other raiders came—a woman and a man with one good arm?

FABIA. Let them kill us, Varro. It doesn't matter. [*Sudden change to feverish eagerness.*] *Did* anyone escape? Any of our people? My husband? One of the children—just one?

VARRO. Some people may have got away . . . not your husband, Fabia. Not any of your children. None of our family. I know; I saw . . . oh, God, I saw . . . help me, now, sister. Our only hope of life is to go away.

FABIA [*hopeless again*]. I'd rather die. I'd rather stay and let them kill us as they killed my family. . . .

VARRO [*sharp*]. They'd kill *me*, Fabia. Not you. [*No reply*.] I'd be no use. I couldn't work with one good arm. They'd kill me to save feeding me. . . . But they are short of women. [*Pause*.] My heart bleeds for you. I know you would rather die than go away. It would have been easier if we had both died. . . . But I didn't die, and—forgive me—I want to live. Don't condemn us both.

FABIA [*with an effort*]. Yes, Varro, I'll come.

VARRO [*seizing the advantage*]. We cannot carry much because of my arm. You will have to be the man of the party.

FABIA [*sudden feeling for him*]. Oh, Varro, your arm. You won't be able to do your lovely metal work. . . . Why did this happen to us?

VARRO [*smouldering anger*]. Because these Northern barbarians are savages. They attack by night. They saw this villa; they wrecked, they stole, they killed—and then moved on to the next place. They've done this all over Africa. . . . [*Calming*.] I'm getting angry and hot, and that is no use to us.

FABIA. I'll get you some water from the fountain.

[*She goes out,* D.L.
[VARRO *continues talking to her.*

VARRO. You can't talk with these savages. There's no common ground. They could have come into the Roman peace. They could have joined us in the peace of Christ. But they made themselves a different Christianity. . . . [*To himself*.] And now there is no peace.

[FABIA *returns with a pitcher of water and a cup.* WANDA *moves into sight, and comes noiselessly forward during the next passages.*

FABIA. Here's the water. . . . Look, I found the little mirror you made me. It was by the fountain. One little thing they didn't destroy.

[*She holds out the mirror. It is polished metal, not glass, shaped like a modern handmirror, with a decorative handle.*]

VARRO. The one your husband asked me to make. It was a pretty piece of work.

FABIA. It still is ... it's not broken. [*Puts the cup in his hand and helps him.*] ... Who are you?

[WANDA *has come up and pushes between them. She jostles them and takes the cup.*

WANDA. I want that water. I want it all. You can't have any of it. It's for my man. Don't touch me, I'm stronger than what you are. My man's asleep. You try any tricks, I'll wake him. Give me the pitcher too.

VARRO [*motioning* FABIA *to do so*]. Certainly. [*To* FABIA, *as* WANDA *puts the pitcher out of their reach.*] There *are* people. I was wrong. Come away, quickly.

WANDA [*seizing* FABIA'*s wrist*]. No, you don't! Not till I let you. Where's the food? You tell me—I'll let you hide. You go down there and hide. [*Pointing* R.] I'll come, and you'll tell me where the food is....

VARRO. Please let go of my sister.... Of course I'll tell you where the food is.... Are there many of you here?

WANDA. I'm not telling. You'd better go. They'll kill you and take your girl.

[*A loud snore from* ATAULF. *They turn and see him.*

VARRO. Yes—we certainly will go. You'll follow us?

FABIA [*terrified but mannerly*]. It will be very kind of you to help us.

[FABIA *and* VARRO *go out,* R.

[ATAULF *gives a mighty snore and wakes himself.*

ATAULF. Here, how can I go to sleep if you snore like that? I've the devil of a thirst.

[WANDA *is quickly at his side with the pitcher, not bothering about the refinements of a cup.*

WANDA. Quick, drink it all before the others come.

[ATAULF *drinks, noisily, then passes the pitcher to* WANDA.

ATAULF. Go on, drink.

WANDA. You have my share.

ATAULF. You've not got a share. You've got what I give you. Do what you're told. Drink.
        [WANDA *drinks, greedily, wiping mouth with back of hand.*
            CARL *and* ODO, *having come in* R., *sneak on them from* U.L.
CARL. I thought so. What about shares? [*Grabs pitcher.*] Nothing left.
    WANDA. It's water. [*Going off* D.L.] There's plenty more through here. [*Calling from off-stage.*] See? There's a fountain. It works. See?   [CARL *follows her, with pitcher.*
CARL [*as he goes*]. Where's this water?
    WANDA. It's lovely, flowing over your wrists. [*Comes back in.*] I like this place. Vineyards like in Spain. We've got water, and we can make wine when the grapes are ripe.
    CARL [*coming back, drinking from pitcher*]. Where are *you* going?
    WANDA [*over* R.] Looking for food.   [*She goes out* R.
ATAULF. Get us some more water, Odo.
            [ODO, *draining the pitcher as he goes, moves out* D.L.
ATAULF. Well, we found the water. Good thing we didn't leave.
CARL. What about the food?
ODO [*off*]. Here, this water comes out of a mouth, like. It's a sort of head. Why's that?
    CARL. To be pretty [*spits*]. Fine sort of leader, you. Fair shares except when we're not looking.
    ATAULF. There was plenty more.
    CARL [*accusing*]. *You* didn't know that when you drank the lot.
    ATAULF. *You'd* have drunk the lot—all right, fight it out?
        [*They begin to get ready for another fight.* ODO *dances in, overgrown schoolboy fashion, splashing water about.*
ODO. Come on, Carl. Have a nice bath.
        [*Pursues* CARL *round the stage with the pitcher, splashing.*
ATAULF. Stop it, Odo. Wasting water...
    ODO. Plenty more. *You* like a wash, too? [*Splashes* ATAULF.] Come on, Carl, better have a wash... [*Chases* CARL *into a corner,* ATAULF *trying to call him off.*] ... Here, where did this come from? [*Looking at pitcher.*] It's not ours.... Here, she got this from somebody. I'm going to look....

[*He runs off* R., *leaving pitcher, and passing* WANDA *in his haste.*]

ATAULF. Wanda! Come here! Where did you get this?

[*Holding up pitcher.*]

WANDA. From the fountain. It's full of water.

ATAULF. I meant this pitcher. Come on, tell. You'd better.

WANDA [*lamely*]. I found it.

ATAULF. Where? Come on, out with it. You'll have to in the end. Who—gave—you—that—pitcher? Don't lie to me, you tramp.

WANDA. She's got soft, useless hands. A thin white face. Just a Roman woman.

ATAULF [*avid*]. Where is she?

WANDA [*desperate*]. She's old. She squints. She's no use....

ATAULF. Where is she?

ODO [*off*]. I've got a prisoner....

CARL. Odo's found somebody.

[*He gives a joyous whoop and rushes off,* R.]

WANDA [*clinging*]. Ataulf, I've been your woman all this time....

ATAULF [*shaking her off*]. Here, you two, wait for me.

[*He, too, goes bounding off* R. FABIA *creeps in round wall.*
WANDA *pounces on her.*]

FABIA. They've found my brother. What shall I do? They'll kill him.

WANDA. Keep your mouth shut or they'll get you too.

FABIA. Please help. You said you'd help.

WANDA. You get behind that pillar and don't breathe, even. They won't look for you till they've killed him. Oh, don't be stupid, what's the good of being alive with one arm? Go on, hide, quick.

[*She hustles* FABIA *behind a pillar. Roars of laughter off.*
ATAULF *bursts in, full of life and energy.*]

ATAULF. Come on! Bring him through here.

[VARRO *is hustled in by* CARL *and* ODO. *The barbarians are happy and united in their favourite occupation.* ODO *grips* VARRO *from the back.* CARL *holds him with one arm but has his knife ready in the other. They bring him to* ATAULF. *This scene should be in gangster mood.*]

CARL. Look what Odo found! Didn't put up a fight.

ODO. Only one good arm...

CARL. Won't have that long——

ATAULF [*interrupting, quietly sinister*]. Who are you? How many of you? Come on, talk. [*Brings his knife closer to* VARRO.] Lost your tongue? Like us to find it for you?

CARL [*with relish*]. I'll find it. This help?

[*Knife at* VARRO's *throat.*

ODO [*producing his knife*]. Or this?

VARRO [*gasping*]. I'll speak if you'll let me.

ATAULF. Ease up. [*They relax their grips but are still dangerously near.*] Talk, Roman. [*In a deadly tone.*] Silence for the noble Roman. This your place?

VARRO. Yes.

ATAULF. Wrong. It's our place.

VARRO. What are you going to do with me?

[*He is trying to establish contact with* WANDA, *but she is impassive.*

ATAULF. You're no use, you see, with one arm.

VARRO. You are going to kill me?

WANDA [*quickly*]. He knows where the food is.

CARL. 'Course. Put you out of your misery. What's the good of you. Ought to have got yourself killed when you smashed your arm.

[FABIA, *agitated, moves into sight.* WANDA *pushes her unceremoniously back.*

VARRO. Give me a few moments to pray. In the name of Christ.

[*A silence.* ATAULF *puts his knife away. So, reluctantly, does* CARL.

ATAULF. He's got us there.

CARL [*frustrated*]. Hell, so he has. What's he want to say that for?

ODO [*almost apologizing*]. We can't kill you, see? Not now you've said that.

VARRO. You are Christians, then? Thank God for that.

CARL [*sulky*]. Sure we're Christians.

ATAULF. Bloody good Christians. Lucky for you... No, we've not done with you yet. We've got things to ask. What's your name?

VARRO. Fabius Varro. An old Roman family. Our people colonized Africa.

ATAULF. Ataulf, Carl, Odo. We're from the North. *We're* colonizing Africa. Where's the food?

ODO. Yes, food, quick.

VARRO. We thought you'd gone. Your friends smashed my arm and left me for dead. That's a month ago. *Hadn't* you gone?

ATAULF. We came back. We like this place. We're staying. You lived here long?

VARRO. All my life, except two visits to Rome.

ATAULF. Then you know where the food is. Where is the food?
[*Standing over him in a menacing attitude.*

VARRO. I'm sorry—the place has been neglected....

ODO/CARL [*stamping in rhythm*]. Food, food, food!

VARRO. I was not in charge of the food. I was a craftsman in metals.... This was my family's villa. That was the great hall, where the pillars are.... We dealt with law and business there...

[*They turn instinctively to look.* WANDA *gives an urgent signal, and* VARRO *looks in the other direction.*
They brought water here and we had bath-houses.

ODO. Like I said. They kept washing themselves.

VARRO. We talked, too. Good talk, it was. Our Roman ancestors made these buildings and terraces, and brought water here, long before my time——

ATAULF [*breaking in, rough*]. Your time's over. We've driven you Romans out, all round the Great Sea. And now find us that food.

VARRO. Will you go away if I find you food?

ATAULF. We're staying. We like this place. Why shouldn't *we* have it?

VARRO. All right, stay. If I find food will you let *us* go?

ATAULF. No! I want the woman.

WANDA [*rushing into the scene*]. Tell him she's no good. *I'm* his woman.

VARRO. She is my sister, Ataulf. She is not for you. You and your friends killed her husband and her children. She mourns them.

ATAULF [*logical*]. If she's lost her man she needs another.... Oh, I see. She's too good for the likes of me? You Romans think you're better than us. You're wrong. You're beaten. You're no good any more. Your women ought to be glad to get us.

VARRO [*stern*]. I don't deny your quality. You live by destruction. You are virile; you are ruthless. We offered you peace—the peace of Rome. But you chose to destroy us. We have seen your work. We see it now. You even destroyed our chapel, though you say you are Christians. It is not the work to please a Roman woman.

ODO [*perky*]. We don't work. We take what we want.

VARRO [*ignoring this*]. *You* seem an intelligent man ...

ATAULF. I'm a hungry man. Your fine speeches are above my head. Roman peace—don't fill my head with Roman nonsense. It's my belly wants filling, and quickly too. Understand?

VARRO. Yes, you express yourself clearly. Now, about filling your belly ...

ATAULF. People don't mock *me*, Roman.

VARRO. Maybe not. But you need food, badly. That boy is famished. I ask you again, may we go? Don't separate us.

ATAULF. Bargaining, eh? Food or woman?

VARRO. Crudely put, but that is the proposition.

CARL. Leave women out of this. Roman women—they aren't much! Food, Ataulf!

ODO [*desperately*]. I *must* have food, Ataulf.

ATAULF [*under pressure*]. All right, find the food.

CARL. And quick, or I'll stop being a Christian and kill you myself.

VARRO [*lighter, no respect for* CARL]. Then you'd never find anything to eat, unless you picked my bones and there's not much on them....

ATAULF [*in a terrible rage, knife out, coming close to* VARRO]. You think we're cannibals? You Roman rubbish, you say that to *my* man? Say your prayers, you one-armed scum——

[CARL *and* ODO *intervene, both speaking at once.*

CARL [*grabbing* ATAULF'*s arm*]. Stop it, you bloody fool ...
ODO [*dragging* VARRO *away*]. Not yet! Not yet!   [*Together.*
CARL. Kill him later. We've got to eat!

ODO. Yes! Wait till we've got the food. [*Struggle.*
ATAULF. Let go of me, I tell you...
[ATAULF *shakes them off. His rage subsides, but he turns his back, glowering.*
VARRO [*regaining his breath*]. I'm sorry I said that. It was a stupid thing to say. I didn't mean it. Of course I shall show you the food stores.
CARL. You'd better.
VARRO. It's a long way. We'd better go now. There's digging.
CARL. Girl can do that.
VARRO. It is much too heavy for the girl. I can't dig with one arm. It will have to be the men. The reserves of food are all buried....
[CARL *and* ODO *look towards* ATAULF *for a lead. He does not turn.*
ATAULF. Go on, you two. I'll look for that woman.
VARRO. It's hard work. [*Apprehensively.*] I'll need all three of you.
ATAULF [*after a short pause, still not turning*]. We'll have to do it. He's got us over this, like he did over being Christians. We'll get our own back. I owe him something back.
VARRO [*pointing right*]. Down there, and follow that wall.
[ODO *and* CARL *rush ahead.* ATAULF, *who is left with* VARRO, *is about to pass him and go off, when he stops.*
ATAULF. No tricks, Roman. It wouldn't be good for you.
[FABIA *appears on the steps.* ATAULF *is facing* VARRO, *back to her.*
VARRO. Oh, if we're speaking would you mind fastening the latchet of my sandal—I'm short of a hand.
[*Puts his foot on a step.*
[ATAULF *looks at him steadily and is about to bend down.*
ATAULF. No tricks? [*He bends down.*
[VARRO *signals to* FABIA *to keep back.*
VARRO. It's a long way, with a loose sandal. Thank you.
[ATAULF *rises, looks around.* WANDA *is apparently concerned with the pitcher. He goes off,* VARRO *following, with a backward glance.*
[WANDA *stands on the steps* L. *and looks out.*

WANDA. All right, come out. He says it's a long way.

[FABIA *comes out and moves* D.R.

What's your name?

FABIA. Fabia.

WANDA. Wanda, they call me. It may be my name. I'm Ataulf's girl. Soldier's bastard, I suppose. Spain, I come from. This lot comes from North, wherever that is. If Ataulf gets you he'll give me to Carl. I hate Carl.

FABIA. I'm afraid he'll kill my brother. Will he? He nearly did just now.

WANDA [*one-track*]. You take my man I'll kill *you*!

FABIA. But I don't want him, Wanda. Or any man. I've lost my man. I only want to go away in peace, with my brother.... You girls go from man to man, you couldn't understand what it is to lose a husband—how could you?

WANDA [*annoyed*]. I *don't* go from man to man. Ataulf's my man. I'll see you don't get him, if I have to kill you. Of course you want him. He's a *man*, not like your feeble brother...

FABIA. I don't want him, Wanda. And my brother isn't feeble. He's injured, that's all.

WANDA. Of course you like Ataulf. You couldn't help it. He's a man. He'd kill anyone who got in his way. He'd kill Carl. Or Odo. Or me, if I didn't stick to him.... You do like him.... Go on, say you like him.... [*Coming close to* FABIA.]

FABIA. He sounds—considerate.

WANDA. You laugh at my man I'll kill you. [*Pushes* FABIA *against a pillar and menaces her.*] You promise you won't take him away from me. Go on, you promise. You're a Roman, you have to keep promises. Go on...

FABIA. Of course I promise. You needn't bully me.

WANDA [*moving away*]. If you break that promise I'll scratch your face and make you ugly. I will. I'm strong. I don't have to behave well like Roman women do. We're not fussed and made pets of like Roman women.

FABIA [*who is making a tremendous effort to keep calm*]. But, Wanda, Roman women aren't made pets of. There's work to do on an African villa. We all have to do our share. We're equals with our men.

WANDA [*blunt*]. That's not sense. Women aren't as good as what men are. We're made to do the heavy work so that they can take life easy between fighting.

FABIA [*patient*]. You're thinking all wrong....

WANDA. Odo said "We don't work," didn't he? That's what *they* think. Some one has to work, with a lot of men on the move. Who? Us women. When Ataulf brought us back here I carried all the food. Else they'd have eaten it all up by the end of the first day.... I've still got some hidden. They'd beat me if they knew.

FABIA [*shocked*]. Oh, how can you bear such a life? Could you come with us, I wonder? You can't stay with this dreadful man.

WANDA. I'm *going* to stay with him. It's only your pretty face I'm afraid of. *I'm* his sort, but you're pretty, and I'm ugly. And if he gets you I'll have to sleep with Carl. I hate Carl.

FABIA [*with a sudden inspiration*]. Wanda, look at yourself.

[*Produces the mirror.*

WANDA [*a child*]. Oooh! May I really hold it? How pretty it is! See how it shines in the light. Look, Fabia. Romans like pretty things, don't they. My man says it's silly, liking pretty things....

FABIA. That's very silly of your man. Oh, Wanda, I'm sorry, I didn't mean to criticize him—but there's no harm in pretty things, you know. My brother made this. That was his work before his arm was injured.

WANDA [*shocked in her turn*]. His *work*? A man? And you said he wasn't feeble!

FABIA. Look at your face in the mirror, Wanda. Now look at me. You're as pretty as I am, and much younger. Would you like to be even prettier?

WANDA [*crying*]. I'm ugly and brown and my hair's tangled and I'm dirty. And you're not fat enough, but you're white and clean and your hair like in those statues.

FABIA. I think I can make you pretty, Wanda. May I try? Then he'd go on liking you. We'd need to wash your face. It won't hurt you. I do it every day.

WANDA. Could you? Would this lovely mirror make me pretty? Oh, I do hope so!

ODO [*off*]. Wanda! Wanda! We've got the food!

WANDA [*changes from excitement to resentment*]. Oh, hell, here comes Odo. Now you'll have to hide and I'll go on being ugly.
   [*She sits, sulky, right foreground.* FABIA *moves towards the pillars but not right out of sight.*
[*Ungraciously.*] Go on, hide.
   ODO [*bursting in*]. Look, we got it! [*Dances round her, taunting her by holding something out of her reach.*] You can't have any. None for you. You didn't help.
   WANDA. I don't want it.
   ODO. All right, don't sulk. I was only teasing. Here, eat it up.
   WANDA. I'm not hungry.
   ODO [*wolfing away at some food*]. Carl's stumping alone; eaten so much he can hardly move. Fancy being old like that. [*Pause.*] Ataulf's wasting time talking to that Roman about how the water comes. [*Laughs.*] It comes all right; what does it matter how? What are *you* sulking about? [*No reply.*] Here, misery, here's news. We're leaving. You and me and Carl. Now we've got enough food. Ataulf wants to stay and grow food when there's all this for nothing. Let him!
   WANDA. We're staying. We're not leaving Ataulf. I'm his girl.
   ODO. Not now he wants that Roman woman. Come on, you be *my* girl! [*Grabs her.*] Give us a kiss.
   WANDA. No! [*Wrenches herself free.*] Ataulf's not having any Roman woman.
   FABIA [*crossing*]. Come along, Wanda, don't let's waste any more time.
                [*She leads* WANDA *to exit* D.L., *and out.*
   ODO. Blow me, the Roman woman.   [*Whistles.*
   [CARL *trudges in, carrying baggage, which he puts down.*
   CARL. Told you to find that girl and get her ready. Where is she?
   ODO. That Roman woman's got her. Says she won't go.
   CARL. She won't *what*? I'm her man now. She'll do what I say.
   ODO. Says we're not quitting Ataulf——
   CARL. What? Stay here and work when there's stores all over Africa for the taking? Ataulf fancies himself. "*My* villa. *My* man." What's he think I am. I don't grow nobody's food. Work for him? Not me. What do *you* want to work for?

F

ODO. I don't want to work. Never said I did.

CARL. All right then, come on. [*Calling.*] Wanda, come on. We're going!

[WANDA *rushes in, in process of hair-dressing,* FABIA *trying to restrain her.*]

FABIA. Wait! Just a minute, Wanda. Let me finish.

WANDA [*attacking* CARL]. You're not to go, you're not to, you're not to...

CARL [*grappling*]. Shut your mouth! [*To* FABIA.] Stay out of it, you! Who told you to make her all fancy? Leave her alone!

FABIA. Let go of that girl! [CARL, *startled, does so.*] Or I'll call your big man. How will he like it if he sees you taking his girl away?

CARL. But, lady, he don't want her no more.

FABIA. That's absurd. She's staying with him. She told me.

CARL [*lame*]. Oh, I thought he was after *you*, lady.

ODO [*daring*]. *You* better come along with us.

[FABIA *just looks at him, without speaking to him.*]

FABIA. Come along, Wanda, we'll finish your hair now.

[WANDA, *equally startled with* CARL, *goes off* L. *with* FABIA.]

ODO [*smug*]. Coo! She put you in your place all right!

CARL. She didn't even answer *you*. If that's a Roman woman Ataulf's welcome. Don't like Roman women. Never did.

ODO. What's she doing now? She's making our girl wash. Maybe she'll make Ataulf wash....

CARL. Odo, what do you say we clear off without Wanda? One less mouth to feed. She's not much. [*Begins to load up with food, etc.*] There'll be other girls. Odo, come on! You carry that lot.... Odo. Just think of those two girls fighting it out for Ataulf. Like to see it... Better go, though, or he'll make us work.

ODO. I don't know...

CARL. You'll just be the boy if you stay. Want to grow up, don't you? Just Ataulf's boy servant...

[ODO, *stung, begins to load up. They have far too much to carry with shields also.*]

ODO. Here, you've given me most to carry.

WANDA [*unable to resist admiration, comes in*]. Look, Carl,

Odo! Look at my hair now! [*Sees the baggage and calls.*] Fabia! Stop them! They really are going! Fabia!

CARL [*to* ODO, U.L.]. I'm the leader. You carry most.

ODO. Who said you were leader? We're the same as each other. Not fair... I'm not just the boy.... [*They go out, wrangling.*]

FABIA [*having come in now*]. Let them go, Wanda. You hated Carl, anyway.

WANDA. They've taken all the food. [*Hysterical.*] What's my man to do when he's hungry?

FABIA [*moved*]. What about yourself, Wanda?

WANDA [*gulping*]. If Ataulf had food he'd give me some.

FABIA. There's plenty more. Don't be worried.

WANDA. You sure? [*Calming down.*] Why weren't you afraid of Carl and Odo? They can be awful rough.

FABIA. I wasn't frightened. It's your man I'm afraid of: I really am.

WANDA [*pleased*]. I know. He's a lovely man to be frightened of.

FABIA. Wanda, look in the mirror now.

WANDA [*doing so*]. Oh! This isn't me. You done something to the mirror?

FABIA. That is you. You stay like that.

WANDA. I didn't know a mirror could make you pretty.... I didn't think he cared what women looked like, till I told him about your white face and soft hands.... I wish *I* had a mirror that made me pretty....

FABIA. It's not the mirror... [*Deciding to humour the idea.*] Well, maybe it is. It made *you* pretty. [*Sudden impulse.*] Wanda, keep the mirror. I'd like you to have it.

WANDA. Me? Me keep this lovely mirror that makes me pretty? For my very own? Oh, no, you can't mean it. I never had a present before. I never had anything pretty of my own before. ... Did your man like you to be pretty?

FABIA [*withdrawn*]. Yes. Men do, you know.

WANDA [*prattling on, excitedly*]. Do they? Now your man's dead I suppose you don't mind what you look like. What's the matter? You want the mirror back?

FABIA [*overwhelmed, near tears*]. I want my husband back.

WANDA. Oh! [*Clumsily attempting comfort.*] I suppose that's

how I'd feel if Ataulf died.... Take the mirror back, Fabia....
No, I can't. I must keep it. It makes me pretty....

FABIA [*very gentle*]. You've never had anything of your own, have you, poor little Wanda? I've had lots of things. Keep the mirror, and stay pretty for your man.

WANDA [*apologetic*]. I only hate you because he wants you....

[VARRO *comes in, from* R.

VARRO. Fabia? Go into the hall and stay there. Ataulf's coming.

WANDA. Go on! Keep out of his sight!

VARRO [*calling, delaying tactics*]. Put some of the food down, Ataulf. You needn't carry all that at once... it won't run away ... not there. Put it by those stones.... Not those stones, the other stones. Out of the sun, man... [*To the women.*] I can't keep this up for long. Please go, Fabia.

[FABIA *goes up steps and through pillars*, L.

WANDA [*to* VARRO]. Look what she gave me. It makes me pretty. See? I'm pretty now. I was ugly before.... The others have gone. They took the food. She says there's more [*a query*].

VARRO. Yes, there's more.... You *are* pretty, indeed! You'd better not let Ataulf see you talking to me. Go and join Fabia.

[WANDA *goes up steps after* FABIA.

[VARRO *goes on calling to* ATAULF, *off* R.

That's one of the stores. When you've eaten I'll show you where we store the grain, so that you can replant....

[ATAULF *lopes in, gnawing*.

You'll *have* to replant, you know. You people think crops grow of their own accord, don't you? You'll need more labour, too. I'm sorry I don't know the details of the water system. You'll have to work them out for yourself.

[ATAULF *grunts and munches*.

When you've seen everything I can show you I want to leave, with my sister and some supplies, as you promised. [*Doubtfully.*] I'm sure you are a man of honour....

[ATAULF *grunts and munches*.

Come along, man, you can stop eating long enough to answer.

ATAULF. I want that woman.

VARRO. Now, look here, you've got a woman of your own.

ATAULF. Ugly tramp I picked up on the march. I want a Roman lady.

VARRO. A Roman lady would make you wash. She'd keep you in order. You'd be a feeble thing like you think I am. Ataulf, you promised——

ATAULF. Promises! Savages don't keep promises. You called me a cannibal.

VARRO. I did apologize.

ATAULF. You and your speeches and your apologies... You just listen, *I'm* going to make a speech.

[*Puts down his food and stands dramatically.*
You noble Romans. You think barbarians are slaves. You used them as slaves, and cut off their girls' hair to make wigs for your ladies. Until you ran short of soldiers. Then you freed the slaves. "You be good little imitation Romans and we won't kill you. We'll send you to war and let our enemies kill you.... Isn't that kind of us Romans?"

VARRO. Ataulf—listen a moment.

ATAULF. Don't interrupt my speech. You wash yourselves, you Romans: you treat your girls soft; you write poetry. But what about the people who *didn't* want to do just what you planned for them, who didn't want to be your slaves or your soldiers....

VARRO. We wanted to civilize your people——

ATAULF. I've not finished my speech.... You wanted to civilize us. Kind of you. What if we preferred our own ways? What if we decided it was time to have *our* share of things? We've come for our share—now. This was your family's villa, all very nice and comfortable. It's ours now. For all your talk about civilization. It's my turn to talk. Rome is finished. [*Peroration.*] The end.

[*He relaxes, and takes a swig from a bottle.*
Hell, I'm thirsty after that great long speech.

VARRO. It was a good speech.

ATAULF [*suspicious*]. You laughing at me?

VARRO. No. Nothing to laugh at. The Romans have been masters a very long time: perhaps it is your turn now.... I wasn't ambitious. I only wanted our villa and our orderly life.... But it's your villa now, as you say. [*Brisk, as though brushing away sadness.*] You'll have to look after it. It needs constant attention. You see what has happened this last month since your raid. It won't run itself. You'll need workers and plans. You won't have time for killing....

ATAULF. You know something? You are talking hard to take my mind off your sister. Where is she? Where's my own girl? Where's Odo and Carl? [*Suspicious, anxious.*] This a trap? You've got some more Romans here? You trying to trick me?

VARRO [*calm*]. Your men have gone. I never thought they would stay and work. You chose Carl badly, and you didn't keep your eye on the boy. You'll have to learn to choose workers.

ATAULF. Bastards! Bloody deserters! I was going to keep them till I got some one better.... *You* did this to me! *You* put this into their heads!

VARRO. Now you know better than that, Ataulf. Of course I didn't. They weren't much good, anyway. The boy could have learned. Maybe he'll find his way back when they quarrel——

ATAULF. You sly one-armed devil, scoring over me again: I'll kill you. Yes, I will. What the hell are you laughing at?

VARRO. Listen, man. They couldn't resist making off with all that food. They didn't stop for *any* of the wine!

[ATAULF *pauses in mid-rage. Suddenly he roars with laughter, clapping* VARRO *on the back.* VARRO *reels a little.*

ATAULF. We got all the wine! Come on, let's drink.

[*He takes another swig from the bottle and makes* VARRO *do the same.* ATAULF *is greedy and noisy.*

ATAULF. Go on, put it down, Roman. Don't be dainty. Drink while we got it. [*Drinks.*] Let's have a drinking-party. Let's get drunk. Let's have a special peace of our own, just you and me, eh? I like you, Varro. Let's stay here together.... Why not?

VARRO. You might not like me to-morrow.

ATAULF. Don't know why you Romans live in Africa when there's Italy.

VARRO. Not enough room. Why don't you people stay in the North?

ATAULF. Not enough room! [*Roars with laughter at the coincidence.*] Same as you. We're alike, you see. Here's your sister at last....

[WANDA *has come out on the steps. She is very self-*

conscious. FABIA *has given her a little Roman drapery. She is posing a little, and looks very attractive in a wild sort of way.* VARRO *smiles approval.* ATAULF *pauses and looks at her.*
She's a beauty.

VARRO. This lady is your own girl.

ATAULF. What? Wanda?

[*He goes across to her, stares a moment, then explodes.*
What have you been doing to yourself? What's your hair like that for? You little tramp, you trying to catch this Roman?

[*Pulls her hair loose.*

VARRO. I'll not have you treat the girl like that.

ATAULF. Stop me, then, with one arm.

WANDA [*coming down*]. No, no, I don't want him. I don't want anyone but you. The Roman lady said if I was pretty you'd keep me. She gave me this. It's a special mirror. It makes me pretty. Look, you can see you're better than the Roman.

ATAULF [*looking at the mirror, simmering down but dangerous in his quietness*]. The Roman lady gave you this? You took it? You didn't ask me about it? What will you do with it?

WANDA [*lulled*]. Keep it for always. It makes me pretty. I wasn't pretty till I had it. Now you'll like me always.

[ATAULF *holds the mirror.*
[*In sudden fear.*] No, no, let me keep it. It's mine. Ataulf, don't break it.

ATAULF. It's another trick.

[*Throws it to the ground and puts his heel on it.*

WANDA. Oh, I loved it so much. It was the only pretty thing I ever had. And now I'll be ugly again.

VARRO [*really angry*]. You bully, what did you do that for?

ATAULF [*to* WANDA]. You listen to me. I'm master here. You ask me before you go taking presents. I don't care whether you're pretty or ugly. I'll keep you while I want you, and then I'll get myself another woman....

WANDA [*breaking away, despairing*]. Ataulf, I'll die if you throw me out. [*She runs off,* R.

ATAULF [*perfectly calm*]. Let's have another drink. What's the matter?

VARRO. Why did you spoil that mirror? She tried to please you and you were brutal and beastly. I hope she leaves you.

ATAULF. What's wrong? [*Mimics.*] "Brutal and beastly." That's how I always treat her. She'll come round.

VARRO [*angry*]. I mistook you for a human being ... and that poor fool loves you, God help her.

ATAULF. Loves me? I suppose she does. I *am* superior to most of our men. You heard I knew history when I made that speech.

VARRO [*sarcastic*]. "Superior to most men." And she's just some one to wait on you, and to be kicked around. She doesn't matter to you——

ATAULF. She's just a girl.... [*Half-grudgingly.*] Well, she's not bad. She's kind. She sticks to me. I'd miss her. [*Sudden outburst.*] And now she's found out she's pretty I'll never be sure of her any more.

VARRO [*light dawning*]. Oh, is *that* the trouble? Marry her, Ataulf. You'd be sure of her then.

ATAULF [*considering*]. Marry Wanda? I never thought of that. Kings and that marry. Not people like me. But a man with a villa ought to be married.... All right, I'll marry her. Could you say the right words?

VARRO. I think so. You'd have to stick to *her*, of course.

ATAULF. Oh, I forgot. No, I won't marry her.

VARRO [*shrugs*]. Just an idea. Why did you spoil her mirror? Girls need pretty things.

ATAULF. Not soldiers' girls. They don't want cluttering up.

VARRO [*firm*]. *All* girls need pretty things. You spoilt her mirror just to be a bully——

ATAULF. Oh, stop nagging, Varro! I'll say I'm sorry. It's bad to pamper them, but I will.... [*Embarrassed.*] Have you another of those mirror things?

VARRO. No, it was special. It was kind of my sister to give it to your girl.

ATAULF [*tentative*]. Make me another?

VARRO. My arm ... How could I?

ATAULF [*holding the mirror, doubtful*]. Could this be mended?

VARRO. No, you were thorough.... I could show you how to

make something.... But you wouldn't want to. Your hands are not made for skilful work.

ATAULF [*brusque*]. Show me.

[VARRO *goes off*, D.L., *talking the while.*

VARRO. I have a few things here which you can use for practice, and there will be some metal in my work-room. She'd treasure it because you made it.

[VARRO *re-enters with a pouch. They take out some things and look at them,* R.C.

ATAULF. Funny you teaching me. Funny there being anything I'd want you to teach me. Good thing I didn't let Carl kill you. *I'm* not like Carl. *I* don't want to kill people all the time....

VARRO. You wanted the food, remember? Never mind. [*Quietly.*] Ataulf!

[ATAULF *looks up from the tools.*

This is our peace—our private and particular peace.

[*For a silent moment the artist and the barbarian look at one another.*

What are you going to make?

ATAULF. Me?

VARRO. Yes, you.

ATAULF. Another mirror?

VARRO. You mustn't expect it to be so good as the last one. I've been working at this longer than you.... You'll have to practise ... you can't rush a craftsman's job. You'll spoil some things. It doesn't matter, and you must not get angry.

ATAULF. I *shall* get angry. Don't take any notice. Make me go on, even if I hit you.... Is she coming? I'd better get this "sorry" business over.

VARRO. Call her.

ATAULF [*calls*]. Wanda! —What shall I say?

VARRO. Say you love her. Tell her you might marry her. Say you are making something, to show that you love her.

ATAULF. Don't soften me up, you Roman.

VARRO. She might find some one gentler. She's pretty, remember.

ATAULF. Huh! You telling *me* how to manage my girl? I'll show you....

[ATAULF *looks very busy as* WANDA *enters. She is tidy, but subdued. She stands before her lord and master and makes the speech she has rehearsed.*]

WANDA. I'm sorry I was bad, Ataulf. I didn't think you'd mind. I'll never take presents again, and I'll never try to be pretty again. I'll always be good if I can stay with you.

[*Silence.*]

VARRO. Well, go on, Ataulf, say something.

ATAULF. Stand over there.

[*Indicates farther to the right.* WANDA *stands where she is told.* ATAULF *then stands in his speech-making position, and speaks aggressively.*]

I'm sorry I broke the mirror. Girls need pretty things. Even soldiers' girls. I was brutal and beastly. I made a mistake. *I made a mistake*, I tell you ... There, Varro, I've apologized. But never again.... What shall I do next?

VARRO. Kiss her. Try to be gentle.

ATAULF. Come over here. [*She obeys.*] He thinks I'm rough with you. He'd have you go all soft and me do the work. Don't you think it. I'm staying the way I am.

WANDA. I don't want you any different. I'll stay while you want me, and then I'll go.

ATAULF. Go, will you? I'm damned if you'll go. I'll marry you, then you'll be trapped. That'll stop any nonsense about going.

WANDA. Ataulf—you're going to *marry* me? Me? Oh, how happy I am.... But you'll be trapped too.

ATAULF. I know. I'll have to put up with it.... Don't go saying you wouldn't mind. If I chase after other women you'd *better* mind. [*Very casual.*] By the way, I'm making you another mirror.

WANDA. *You* are? But you can't make mirrors.

ATAULF. Who says I can't? He's showing me. Mine will be better than his, of course.

VARRO. You'll get the last of the light if you take it through that way. [*Indicates steps* R.] I'll come and help you in a few minutes.

[ATAULF *and* WANDA *move over* R.

WANDA. Will this one make me pretty too, like the other one did? Shall I be able to go on being pretty?

ATAULF [*the master*]. Just you listen, Wanda. I don't like women to be dirty, untidy sluts. You remember that. Stay as you are now. Don't change yourself. Not at all. You stay pretty, my girl, or I'll belt you.

VARRO [*weary*]. Ataulf, tell the girl you love her. Make her happy, for God's sake.

WANDA. But he *does* make me happy! [*Laughing.*] Can't you see that, you silly Roman fool?

ATAULF [*bullying*]. Now then, you stop laughing at my friend. He's got feelings, same as you have. You little savage, laughing at civilized people ... Come on. I'll teach you to laugh at my friend.... [*They go off.*

VARRO [*quite still, spent*]. Your friend—for a minute in history. And what comes next?

[FABIA, *moving swiftly but not running, comes to him and wipes his forehead. They come down* R.C.

FABIA. Varro, I listened. I'm afraid. We must go while he is not thinking about us. Let's go now, brother.

VARRO [*speaking with eager but low intensity*]. No. I can't go yet—I've work to finish. I'm teaching him to make a mirror. [*Sitting.*] It's ironic, isn't it? His knife was within an inch of my throat—and I'm teaching him to make a mirror.

FABIA. Don't trust him. He's a killer.

VARRO [*as before*]. But he's making something. He's wondering. He's interested in how the villa's run; in the water supply. We're both men, Fabia, and we find we can talk to each other.

FABIA. Look around you. Look what they've done, this man and his friends....

VARRO. Our Roman life is past. He's part of the future. God help him if he has to start right at the beginning. God help all newcomers if they have to start at the beginning. I must do what I can for him—for the future.

[*A loud curse from* ATAULF, *off* R.

FABIA [*serious*]. The future, Varro. Cursing and violence and destruction.

VARRO [*very quiet and matter-of-fact, flat*]. He may have cut a finger. A Roman might curse if he cut his finger. I'll go and see.

[*He gets up and moves* R.

[*Very serious.*] Dear Fabia, you who have suffered beyond hope, let me go on hoping. Let me keep alive this peace between him and me. . . .

FABIA. What peace, brother? The Roman peace is dead—they killed it. What peace, after Rome?

VARRO [U.R. *now*]. Let me try to find out. [*He goes,* R.

[FABIA *picks up the piece of window-framing, and as she speaks she absently breaks off pieces.*

FABIA [*again*]. What peace, brother, after Rome?

[*She has reduced the framing to an upright, a cross-bar, and a short upright at one end of the cross-bar. It is now a cross, except for the one extra upright. Suddenly she looks at it and sees what she has done. She deliberately breaks off the short piece, so that now she holds a cross.*

[*Strong.*] Oh, God, could it be this peace?

The CURTAIN *falls.*

Genius Loci

By Sagittarius

For
NATALIE

© *Sagittarius* 1964

CHARACTERS

WILL, *a Stratfordian*
DR OLIVER, *an Oxfordian*
MR POTTER, *a Baconian*
PROFESSOR TITMUSS, *a Marlovian*
BERT, *a Statistician*
MARIAN HART, *a Thespian*
SEXTON

Members of a Shakespearian Company. Only four of the Players are named, but others can join the song and dance if desired.

The action of the play occurs in the churchyard of Holy Trinity Church, Stratford-on-Avon.

TIME: *The early hours of April 23, 1964.*

Applications regarding amateur performances of this play should be addressed to Messrs Samuel French, Ltd, 26 Southampton Street, Strand, London, W.C.2, or Samuel French Inc., 25 West 45th Street, New York.

Genius Loci

The portico and church door, U.R. *Trees cast heavy shadows on the moonlit scene. As the curtain rises, an owl hoots. The clock strikes four. The* SEXTON *enters with a lantern. He searches on the ground for a lost object. A dog barks.*

SEXTON. Quiet! Here, Toby, here! Good dog; good dog. [*Barking.*] Sssh! You noisy brute. D'you want to wake the whole of Stratford? What good are you if you can't help me find my key, hey?

[*The owl hoots, the dog barks again.* Stop barking at the owl! He don't give a hoot for you. [*Looking up.*] Do you, my friend? [*To dog.*] See? [*Searching.*] Oh, where's it got to, that blamed key? No good looking for lost things in the dark. I'll away to my bed. Come on, Toby! Home! [*Barking.*] Stop that noise! Do you hear me? [*As he goes.*] Toby! Toby! I'm after you. You'll catch it. I'll give you what for.

[*He exits* D.L., *as* DR. OLIVER *enters stealthily* U.R. *A typical schoolmaster of sixty, precise, punctilious, kindly but somewhat condescending. He carries two crow-bars tied together with strips of canvas. He stands listening. Toby barks in the distance.*

OLIVER [*whispering*]. It's all right, Marian, he's gone. You can come out now.

[MARIAN *enters, carrying a powerful electric lantern. She is twenty, spirited and attractive. She wears a long coat over a summer frock.*

Be careful, don't show that light! [*She switches it off.*] That's better. Now where's the professor?

MARIAN. I don't know; he must be somewhere.

OLIVER. Of course he must be somewhere. No need to state the obvious. [*Calls softly.*] Titmuss! Titmuss!

MARIAN. Ssh! That old man may come back.

TITMUSS [*off, plaintively*]. Coming—I'm coming as fast as I can. [*A dull thump.*] There, I've dropped it. Oh, dear me! I can't see. Oliver, where are you?

MARIAN. Wait a minute, Professor! I'm coming.

OLIVER. No, stay here! He'll get out of it himself.

MARIAN. Heavens, that dog scared me stiff. Who was it, do you think?

OLIVER. Oh, some watchman on his rounds. But I shouldn't have run away, you know. I should have passed the time of night with him. After all, we're not small boys robbing an orchard, nor trespassers, by sitting in a churchyard.

MARIAN. But we will be when we get into the church.

OLIVER. Not even then, strictly speaking. I am perfectly prepared to pay my sixpence admission.

[TITMUSS *enters. He is a pedantic old fusspot, carrying camera, flashlight, and umbrella.*

TITMUSS. Sixpence? I'd give six pounds to be out of this boneyard. Dropped the camera, twisted me ankle, lost me glasses.

OLIVER. Come, Titmuss, brace up! You can't be a casualty now.

TITMUSS. Oh, dear me, no. Far from it. Stratford, we are here! "This is the night that either makes me or foredoes me quite." ... Marlowe.

OLIVER. Marlowe? Never in life! Let's make a start, Titmuss, we don't want to be surprised again.

MARIAN. We do look a bit odd with all this gear. Not to say highly suspicious.

TITMUSS. Not in the least—we might be American tourists sitting up all night for the Birthday mysteries.

OLIVER. Misguided pilgrims, paying homage to the wrong man, in the wrong place, on the wrong day.

TITMUSS. Or we might be naturalists catching moths, or nocturnal birdwatchers.

MARIAN. But we're not; hence the guilty conscience.

TITMUSS. Guilty conscience? Dear me, no. We're not meditating a felony... it may come under the category of... let me see... not a misdemeanour, certainly, but perhaps, maybe, a technical offence.

MARIAN. What! Breaking into tombs? Well, I'd rather be catching moths myself. This isn't part of my job.

OLIVER. God forbid it should be mine. But if it is an offence, whose fault's that? I've begged and prayed for an exhumation order long enough.

TITMUSS. In any civilized country in the world the State helps research.

MARIAN. Yes, in libraries, not graveyards.

TITMUSS. My dear, you don't understand.

MARIAN. Well, what do you expect? I'm not a scholar, only an actress.

OLIVER. Of course, they opened Spenser's tomb, and Marlowe's. Why not this? For goodness' sake, Marian, don't start dithering at this point. Just think, behind that door lies the answer to the whole trumped-up Shakespeare mystery.

MARIAN. What! You mean there's no mystery?

TITMUSS. Of course not, the man was Marlowe.

OLIVER. He was the Earl of Oxford.

TITMUSS. Perfect nonsense!

OLIVER. Allow me to remind you, you were an Oxford man before you got the American Marlowe craze. And before that, a fanatical Baconian.

TITMUSS. Well, I'm always open to reason. I say, leave no tombstone unturned.

OLIVER. You're a weathercock.

TITMUSS. And you're a pigheaded bigot. As for your cheap sneers at American discoveries, admit it took an American to put Marlowe on the map.

OLIVER. Well, he's off the map now.

MARIAN [*sharply*]. Look! What's over there?... Oh, nothing ... [*She shivers.*] Ooh, it's so terribly quiet... but thrilling too. Like a first night, with the stage all set... waiting for some one ... but who?

OLIVER. Now don't start seeing things, my dear!

MARIAN. Who wouldn't, in a graveyard at four in the morning? Do let's go inside.

OLIVER. Well, come along! What are we waiting for? [*To* TITMUSS.] I'll take the tools, you hang on to the camera, and she'll hold the light. By the way, where's the key? You've got it.

TITMUSS. Fair Marian shall be my torchbearer.

OLIVER. You've got the key, Titmuss. Where is it?

TITMUSS. Oh, dear me, yes, of course. I abstracted it from the door when the sexton wasn't looking.   [*Giggles.*

MARIAN. Ssh!

OLIVER. Where is it?

TITMUSS [*producing key*]. I knew it! I told you so.

    [MARIAN *switches on lantern and they go up to the door.*

OLIVER. Open it, then!... What's the matter? Doesn't it fit?

TITMUSS. Of course it fits. It's gone in perfectly easily.

OLIVER. Then turn it.... You must be turning the wrong way.

TITMUSS. No, no, I *have* turned it.

OLIVER. Well, *push* it.

TITMUSS. I *am* pushing. .. The thing's stuck. It's stuck.

OLIVER. The key's stuck?

TITMUSS. No, the door. It won't open; it's fastened.

OLIVER [*after pushing*]. You've made a hash of it. It's the wrong key.

TITMUSS. Kindly allow me to tell you, in words of one syllable, I took *this* from *that* and placed it *here* where it has been till now.

OLIVER [*taking key and replacing it in door*]. All right. Now let us think calmly... reconstruct. The sexton missed the key at closing-time, so he bolted the door.

MARIAN. From the inside. That must be it.

TITMUSS. Then how did he get out?

OLIVER. Ah, by another door! So, he came back to look for the key. That's what he was doing.

TITMUSS. Well, then, obviously we must look for another door.

MARIAN [*starting*]. What was that?

OLIVER. Just bats flying around... Put out the light. Come on.

MARIAN [*as they go off* L., *stealthily*]. Ooh, I hope there are no flying buttresses.

[*The owl hoots again.* POTTER *steals in* R. *He is a heavy, slow-witted, disputatious type, with an aggressive manner. He carries a rucksack, field-glasses, and a lantern.*

POTTER. Wait a minute! Stay there! I'll have a look. [*Straightens up.*] Coast's clear. I could have sworn I heard voices.

[BERT *appears, weighed down with two cases. He is young, laconic, dead-pan, and well dressed. He unloads, looks round, whistles in amazement.*

POTTER. What are you gaping at?

BERT. Lovely, isn't it? A fair picture.

POTTER. Picture, ha! All Stratford's a picture. Tarted-up fake. Bogus Birthplace. Picture-postcard High Street. The Shakespeare Head, the Shakespeare Hotel, the Shakespeare bunk.

BERT. So what? It's reely beautiful.

POTTER. And here's the sacred Burial Place. Holy mumbo-jumbo! Here lies Shakespeare, under his lying monument... that simpering sheepshead! How I'd like to see it tarred and feathered—with the plumes of the "Swan of Avon."

BERT. The Swan of Avon? Never heard of it.

POTTER. Don't ask me to pursue the revolting subject. Just do what we came for.

BERT. O.K. Where do we start? [*Moves to door.*] Why, there's a key here. That's a break... Something funny, though.

POTTER. What's the matter?

BERT. It turns all right, but it won't open.

POTTER. Well, force it! [*Reaching into his rucksack.*] I came prepared for this. Here's a jemmy... Well?

BERT. A bit of a job with that thing. They made doors solid then.

POTTER. Well, think of something, can't you?

BERT. Maybe there's another way in.

POTTER. All right, come on.

BERT. We don't want to lug all this stuff around.

POTTER. Or be overtaken by daylight, either. By the way, how long will you need for the job?

[OLIVER *appears on the other side of the portico.*
[*He listens, unseen.*

BERT. Don't know exactly. There's the box to fix and hide, the wires to run. Maybe fifteen minutes; maybe more.

POTTER. As long as that? Well, it's up to you. Everything depends on split-second timing. Remember, it's dynamite.

BERT. No problem. Leave it to me.

POTTER. All right. I'll go first, I've got the lantern.

BERT. Don't show a light till we get in. You never know, you know.

POTTER. Keep behind me. Watch your step! [*They go off*.

OLIVER. Good Lord! Dynamite!! And Potter here. You saw him?

TITMUSS [*entering*]. No mistake about that; it was Potter in the flesh.

MARIAN [*entering*]. Did you hear that? Ooh! He's going to blow up the church. [*Horrified, moves towards box.*

OLIVER. Not before I've opened the tomb if I know it. Marian, keep away! It might go off.

TITMUSS. Indeed it might. I've had enough, Oliver. *I'm* not going to be blown up, oh, dear me, no.

OLIVER. Don't lose your head! They haven't got it inside yet. I'll be there first.

TITMUSS. Not with me. You can't, anyway, with all the doors fast. I know. I've got an idea.

OLIVER. What?

TITMUSS. Let's come back to-morrow. If the church is still here, that is. I'll hide somewhere. Don't you think so, Marian?

OLIVER [*unwrapping the canvas round the crowbars*]. No. Titmuss, it's now or never. Don't you understand? This is *the* Birthday eve. People won't be so excited about the great whatsit for a hundred years. My revelation will be world news to-morrow —with radio, Press, the lot—and I'm not putting it off for anyone. We're breaking in.

TITMUSS. Now, look here, Oliver, look here! Listen to me! I don't mind sacrilege—if you leave the tomb, exactly as you found it—but breaking and entering, no, no, no! [*He sits on steps.*

OLIVER. Then what about you, Marian? You won't let me down. It needs more than one pair of hands.

MARIAN. All right, I'll do my best. [*Takes crowbar, then stops and listens.*] No use. They're coming back, I can hear them.

[*She puts lantern on steps.*]

OLIVER. Never mind. I'll get rid of Potter. I'll shake him.

MARIAN. Ssh! They're coming. [*Puts down crowbar.*]

TITMUSS. Enter two gravediggers too many.

BERT [*reappearing*]. Well, you see for yourself, Mr Potter, we've had it. A spot of cracksmanship is indicated.

POTTER [*entering*]. Go ahead, then. Get on with it. [*Seeing the others at the door he stops dead.*] What the hell's all this? So it's you, Oliver. I might have known it.

OLIVER. Well, if it isn't Mr Horatio Potter, groping in the dark as usual.

POTTER [*furiously*]. I suppose a man may take a walk at night without being challenged. What is this? An ambush?

OLIVER. You flatter yourself. I'd walk miles to avoid you.

TITMUSS. I might say "ill-met by moonlight," to quote Marlowe.

POTTER. Bacon, you old fool!

OLIVER. The Earl of Oxford, you mean.

BERT [*to* MARIAN]. Who are they talking about? They're crazy. I'm getting on with it. [*Goes up to door,* OLIVER *following him.*

OLIVER. Here, stop that!

BERT. I beg your bloody pardon! [*Disregarding him.*] Shall I bring the stuff in?

POTTER. Yes, yes.

[*Makes for door,* BERT *moves to pick up box.*

TITMUSS [*agitated*]. No, no ... don't ... you can't. Stop it! [*To* MARIAN, *sotto voce.*] They're going to blow it up.

OLIVER [*to* POTTER]. The door's bolted, you can't get in.

POTTER. We'll see about that. [*Tries door, then swings round.*] Is this some sort of a damn silly game?

OLIVER. Game? I'd hate to be *your* playmate, Mr Potter.

BERT [*to* POTTER]. Well, how about it? When do we start?

TITMUSS. Who's this? Your First Murderer?

POTTER. He's my technical consultant.

TITMUSS. A technical consultant? [*Looks at box.*] God help us!

BERT. I'm working with a computer.

MARIAN [*to* BERT]. Well, no one's introducing us, but I'm Marian Hart, a research assistant—temporary. Actually I'm an out-of-work actress.

BERT [*shaking hands*]. Pleased to meet you.

TITMUSS. Computer! You mean, an adding-machine?

[*Laughs.*

BERT. What's so funny, ha, ha?

POTTER. You merely display your ignorance by jeering at modern techniques.

OLIVER. I can only deduce that your calculating faculty has become deranged by adding up all those anagrams, ciphers, acrostics, and digits, so you hand over stylistic problems to a machine.

POTTER. And I can only deduce you have never heard of statistical analysis.

BERT. Stands to reason. It's perfectly simple. We set the text up in binary (that's what Mr Potter gives me), five bits to a ward—and of course we've already got the perameters of central tendency. Then, whatever you feed in, the apparatus does its stuff. For instance, Shakespeare gets sorted out...

TITMUSS. And comes out Bacon! [*Tittering.*] Mr Potter's sausage machine. The last word in scholarship. Prospero appealing to Caliban.

BERT. Prospero! Caliban! Who are they? I don't get it.

OLIVER [*to* POTTER]. Who can seriously suppose critical judgment will be influenced by mechanical gadgets?

BERT. You can't argue with facts. No need to do your nut over who or what. [*To* MARIAN.] Now, who do *you* back?

MARIAN. Frankly, I couldn't care less who wrote the plays, so long as I can act in them.

BERT. Now that's talking. Tell me more about you. And about Prospero and Caliban.

MARIAN. I'd love to—if you'll tell me about [*looks at box*] your computer. [*They move into the shadows.*

OLIVER. Well, Mr Potter, now we have exchanged civilities, don't let me detain you. [*Sits on steps.*

POTTER. I'm obliged for the hint, but I've no intention of going. I thought *you* were. [*Sits on steps. Puts lantern down.*

OLIVER. Wishful thinking. You won't sit me out if we stay here till Doomsday.

TITMUSS. The only sensible thing is obviously for us all to depart. [*Sits on steps.*] We'll look pretty silly in the morning when they find us here with this incriminating impedimenta.

POTTER. Doubtless you have some nefarious purpose in mind, but you won't steal a march on me.

OLIVER. I was here first.

POTTER. That doesn't give you any prior right.

OLIVER. I've a moral right to resent your intrusion.

POTTER [*rising*]. Intrusion! Since you've said it, I resent yours on more serious grounds.

OLIVER. What grounds?

POTTER. You have invaded the field of the Shakespeare controversy.

OLIVER. Indeed! Is that your private property, your preserve, your copyright?

POTTER. In so far as we presented proof fifty years ago that Francis Bacon is Shakespeare.

OLIVER. Proof? I've got fifty times better proof that he is the Earl of Oxford.

TITMUSS. And fifty years hence all the world will accept my proof, that he's Christopher Marlowe.

OLIVER [*impatiently*]. Marlowe? A corpse? A dead man can't write one play, let alone twenty-five.

TITMUSS. Dead? That's the story, but Christopher Marlowe never died by the dagger in Deptford, but was smuggled abroad as one of Sir Thomas Walsingham's secret agents ... Sir Thomas Walsingham, and we all know who he was—head of the Secret Service.

POTTER. Yes, and we all know what they found in his tomb—nothing.

TITMUSS. And nothing's what you'll find in Bacon's. Nothing! Take my word for it.

OLIVER. Don't start on Bacon now, Titmuss. And you know my view of *your* Marlowe theory—balderdash!

POTTER [*to* OLIVER]. No more than yours.

OLIVER. Everyone's entitled to his own opinion.

POTTER [*rising*]. But no one that calls himself a scholar is entitled to reduce a matter of world importance to the level of irrelevant imbecility. The disclosure of the undoubted author commands respect, but the wanton introduction of a horde of impossible claimants merely invites ridicule.

OLIVER [*picking up crowbars*]. So? This is the end. I've had enough. Come on. [*To* TITMUSS.] Take this!

[*Gives bar to* TITMUSS.

TITMUSS. What are you doing?

POTTER. Don't think you can move me by threats or violence! Where's my jemmy? You can't frighten me. [*Feels in rucksack as* OLIVER *and* TITMUSS *go to door*.] Albert! Albert! [*Sees jemmy lying on steps*.] Here it is. [*Goes towards door*.] I can defend myself.

OLIVER. Stay out of this! Get away!

BERT [*reappearing with* MARIAN]. What's up? What's going on here, a free fight?

POTTER. Now, do your worst, both of you! I am armed.

OLIVER. Keep off! Mind your own business!

TITMUSS. I'll stand between you. Take care, Potter!

BERT [*to* MARIAN]. What are they fighting about?

MARIAN. Doctor Oliver's trying to get in.

BERT. So are we. Come on! [*They make for the door. To* OLIVER.] That's not the way. Give it here! [*Tries to take crowbar*.] Give it to me!

[*Takes bar from* TITMUSS.

OLIVER. You keep out of it!

POTTER [*taking bar from* ALBERT]. No, no, I can manage this. Get the gear and then follow me in.

BERT [*moving to take box*]. If you say so; but you won't get that door open without me.

TITMUSS [*to* BERT]. Stop, stop I tell you! You can't do this, it's criminal! I won't have you blowing up the church. Leave that infernal machine!

BERT. Infernal machine! What are you talking about?

MARIAN. He means it's a bomb...

BERT. Don't make me laugh! That's my tape-recorder.

[*Turns switch on machine.*

POTTER. It's more than a bomb. Just wait till this blasts off in the middle of the service. Hear the voice of truth!
  [*There issues from the tape-recorder a fanfare of trumpets, followed by a stentorian voice:*

>   Bacon is Shakespeare,
>   Shakespeare a sham,
>   Stratford a whited sepulchre,
>   The Birthplace bogus,
>   The legend a racket.
>   Stop the rot!
>   Learn the truth!
>   Bacon is Shakespeare!
>   Bacon is Shakespeare!

  [*The door is opened very slowly from inside.*
MARIAN. Look! The door! It's opening. The door!
  [BERT *switches off. All turn and face the portico in dead silence. A thrush sings. Then all back into the shadows as the figure of* WILL *appears, dressed in doublet and hose, and lighted by a golden glow from the lanterns on the steps. He shades his eyes and peers into the darkness.*
WILL. Who's there? Night-prowlers, robbers and ruffians! Show yourselves! Do you knock and run away?
OLIVER [*with a gasp*]. Why, it looks like... it can't possibly be——
TITMUSS [*agitated*]. Don't answer, for God's sake!
POTTER. Look at the clothes.
WILL. Whisper as you may, I hear you well.
Come out, and let me see your hangdog faces,
Or shall I drag you into the light? You rogues,
I'll have you answer for disturbing my sleep.
OLIVER. Let go of me, Titmuss. I'll speak to him.
TITMUSS. No, no. I don't like this, it's uncanny.
OLIVER [*advancing towards* WILL]. I... we... were taken by surprise. Not knowing... expecting you... anyone would be here. I mean, people don't usually sleep in church.
WILL. Do not the dead sleep here? Have they no right
To a little peace before the Day of Judgment?
OLIVER. Er... of course... but nothing on earth can wake the dead.

WILL. Is that then reason to awaken one
Who may desire to pass the night in church
So as to be up betimes? Is there no rest,
No sanctuary in consecrated ground?

OLIVER. I ... er ... we had no intention of breaking your rest; and I assure you we aren't ruffians or robbers, but respectable citizens. A schoolmaster, a professor, and a philologist ... and our helpers.

[*As he names them the others emerge from the shadows.*]

WILL. Then, good Master Pedant and reverend Doctor,
I, Will, actor of Stratford, ask what's your business?
If you are honest, I am the more amazed,
As you should be ashamed, by your misconduct.

OLIVER. On my honour, our purpose was peaceable.

WILL. Had you not broken the peace, I'd have my sleep out.

OLIVER. Again, I apologize most sincerely. It was all a fuss about nothing, I beg you to let it pass. I can only say that now we have inadvertently broken your sleep, I would be sorry to keep you from your breakfast.

WILL. No matter, sir, I always fast till daybreak.
Besides, I am here awaiting company
For our solemnities on St George's Day.

[*He sits on steps.* OLIVER *rejoins the others.*]

BERT. We could rush him; we're four to one. What say?

OLIVER. I'll try persuasion first.

TITMUSS. Yes, go on, Oliver!

OLIVER [*approaching* WILL]. I see you are in no haste, but our time presses; and now you know we are not ruffians, my friends and I would like to go inside if we may.

WILL [*rising*]. By all means—if for prayer and meditation. It is too early yet for Divine Service.

TITMUSS. It is best to visit churches when no one's about if one wants to examine the building at leisure.

WILL. One may seek salvation in the dark,
Not architecture. There's no light inside.

OLIVER. I seek truth, and that's a way to salvation, they say.

WILL. Where hides truth here that must be sought by night?

POTTER. Nowhere here. This fabric is dedicated to falsehood.

TITMUSS. The better the place the worse the fraud.
WILL. What fraud? What falsehood? You speak in riddles. Be plain!
OLIVER [*bluntly*]. Then, sir, in plain terms, it is my purpose to exhibit the so-called Shakespeare as a fraud by opening his so-called tomb.
WILL. A damnable purpose leading to damnation.
The hand is cursed that dares to touch the grave.
TITMUSS. Cursed! I know that curse by heart:

> "Goode friend for Jesus' sake forbeare
> To digge the dust enclosed here.
> Blest be ye man that spares these stones,
> And curst be he that moves my bones."

Most execrable doggerel, and by a later hand.
WILL. It serves its purpose—to deter grave-robbers.
POTTER. It marks the end of a false trail.
TITMUSS. It is a signpost deliberately pointing in the wrong direction—that is to say, a pointer to the Shakespeare mystery. He is somebody else.
WILL. I must confess I'm greatly mystified.
If he's not buried here, where is he buried?
And if he's not himself, who may he be?
POTTER. Why, he's Francis Bacon.
TITMUSS. Nonsense; he's Christopher Marlowe.
OLIVER. He is the Earl of Oxford—and others.
WILL [*laughing*]. A many-headed poet. Here's a prodigy.
MARIAN [*to* BERT]. He's making fools of them all. I never thought them so ridiculous before.
TITMUSS [*to* WILL]. I do beg you to pay no attention to these people. As for authorship, only Marlowe fills the bill.
OLIVER [*to* WILL]. He filled a grave long before most of the plays were ever written.
POTTER. Bacon alone lived long enough to write them all...
WILL. Excepting Shakespeare, who also lived long enough.
OLIVER. Out of the question. The Stratford man's claim is preposterous....
TITMUSS. Definitely impossible.
POTTER. Absolutely absurd.

WILL. Why so absurd, preposterous, and impossible?

OLIVER. Whoever wrote the plays must have been a courtier, which the Stratford man was not, and Oxford was.

POTTER. And he must have been a lawyer, which the Stratford man was not, but Bacon was.

TITMUSS. Also a soldier and a traveller, which the Stratford man was not, but Marlowe was.

MARIAN. And by this reasoning, he must, from his knowledge of femininity, have been a woman, which he was not.

OLIVER. But the Countess of Pembroke was ...

MARIAN. But don't forget Queen Elizabeth ... or was she?

WILL. Would you agree he must have been a poet?

OLIVER. Yes, and the greatest—but misnamed.

TITMUSS. Oh, dear me, yes, the prince of poets.

WILL. If so, might he not, rubbing shoulders with courtiers,
Brush off their bloom? or hobnobbing with lawyers,
Acquire their jargon? and from travellers' tales
Glimpse far lands through their eyes, and paint them too,
Snatch from grammarians some Latin scraps,
Or even learn a little to construe?
And ape the quips of University wits?
Then, gathering these crumbs, Autolycus-like,
Serve them to salt imagined conversations?
And as for being woman to write of women,
Has not each man enough of his mother in him?

MARIAN. Well argued, Will. [*To* OLIVER.] How will you answer that?

OLIVER. I am the last to deny the power of imagination; all I say is that the Stratford man was no poet.

POTTER. How could he be? You have only to look at the place in Tudor times—a miserable hamlet, a filthy cattle-market, a pig-sty. What could it breed but a country bumpkin, an illiterate lout?

TITMUSS. He was never even a page in a great house; he was a butcher's boy.

WILL. The more's the wonder he was named as playwright.

POTTER. Everything we know of him contradicts his poetical character.

WILL. Does Bacon's character support his claim?

MARIAN. Certainly, if a great thief is more poetical than a little poacher.

WILL [*to* OLIVER]. Does your claim rest on Oxford's character?

OLIVER. His conduct was undoubtedly more befitting to a poet.

MARIAN. No doubt of that, if a noble waster is more poetical than a thrifty showman.

WILL. The poet shows in his work, not in his biography.

POTTER. A lifelong study of the plays reveals them as the work of a man of birth and breeding.

WILL. Only a simpleton thinks favourites of fortune
Alone are favourites of the heavenly Muse.
For Aesop was a slave, and matchless Horace
The son of a slave, and Terence was a slave,
Plautus, a menial servant; and our famed Chaucer,
A vintner's son, Spenser, the son of a journeyman.
Kyd's father was a scrivener, Webster's a tailor,
And John Donne was the child of an ironmonger.

TITMUSS. And Marlowe, of a shoemaker, I grant you that, oh, dear me, yes. But he entered College, becoming a Master of Arts of Cambridge. A poor boy may become a scholar and a gentleman but only if he attends the University. All the rest must stick to trade.

WILL. But no man's bound to follow his father's business,
Or stay where he was born. A native of Stratford
Is free to choose as his adopted country,
Blackfriars, Illyria, Southwark, what you will,
And choose the trade of poet, and find a market
For wares not measured by yards, or weighed in pounds.

POTTER. He can also choose to present the work of others as his own—for a consideration, lending his unworthy name as a screen for his betters.

WILL. In what his betters, sharing a shameful secret?

OLIVER. Every one knows that great personages concealed their association with rogues and vagabonds of the stage.

POTTER. Oh, I admit the Stratford man did a flourishing trade blackmailing his patrons.

WILL. He kept his bargain, if their secret was buried with him.

MARIAN. He only cheated them by becoming immortal. They hid their shame behind his glory; now you'd build their glory on his shame. [*Will smiles at her.*

BERT. Fair's fair, that's what I say. Credit where credit is due.

POTTER. Exactly; that's what makes identification imperative.

OLIVER. The world waits for us to tear off the mask and show the true face.

WILL. But dare you claim, on your conscience as scholars,
These comedies, these tragedies and histories
Were thrown off in a nobleman's idle hours,
Or in snatched moments by a busy statesman?
You dare not say so! Then, go chase another
Signor Incognito or Lord Anonymous!

MARIAN. What he means to tell you is that Shakespeare's a professional.

BERT. Well, he's got something there. We're back where we started; it might be anyone.

MARIAN. Anyone—so long as he's a peer of the realm.

WILL. How can you hide that Bacon loathed the stage,
And Oxford shamed to lend his name to it?

TITMUSS. But Shakespeare left it. Remember that! And left no mention of his works in his will.

WILL. He'd left the plays beforehand to the players,
They, sole possessors and his natural heirs.

POTTER. Not for all time; they are our national heritage, which the concealed author addressed to an audience of higher intelligence. They belong to the domain of literature.

WILL. So when you find the legacy of value,
Abolish the testator. Take away
The play from the actor, the actor from the play.
But know you well, we'll never yield our title.
This poet chose the Playhouse for his study,
His college, workshop, battlefield and kingdom,
Whose air his creatures breathed, whose boards they trod,
And call to witness—these originals.
Look to yourselves. Here comes my company.
[*Raising his voice.*]
Appear, Master Burbage! I wait you, Master Kempe.

To me, Master Condell. Show yourself, Master Hemynge!
> [*As they are named, the members of the Globe Company enter* R., *and* L., *and stand. They are in costume, with flowers in their hats, and carry green branches.*

Welcome, old friends, on this St George's Day,
To our accustomed games. But first, deal fairly
With these unwelcome, mischievous intruders
Caught in the very act of sacrilege.
Grave-robbers, evil-wishers, greybeard ghouls,
Foes to this ground, invaders of our haunts,
Witless in argument as they are rude,
Disdaining Shakespeare and our fellowship.
Away with them! Let them be exorcized!

MARIAN. Oh, please, Will, please don't exorcize me. I would be one of you. [WILL *smiles at her.*

> [*The Players dance in a ring round* OLIVER, TITMUSS, POTTER, *and* BERT *while singing the following lines to the tune of the Fairies' Song, from "The Merry Wives of Windsor," Act V, Scene V.*

> Fie! Fie! Fie! Fie!
> Fie on foolish vanity,
> Fie on wicked heresy,
> Beat the rascals till we tire,
> Thrash them for offences dire,
> Chase them out of Warwickshire!
> We of Shakespeare's company,
> Beat them for discourtesy.
> Pinch them and thrash them and turn them about
> Till candles and starlight and moonlight be out.

> [*The Players dance off into the church,* WILL *last as the* SEXTON *enters, trailing a string of coloured pennons.* MARIAN *has slipped off unnoticed. The door closes.*
> OLIVER, TITMUSS, POTTER, *and* BERT *stand as if stunned.*

SEXTON. Good day, gentlemen, good day. You're early comers, but there won't be no service yet awhile.

BERT. They can't do that to me. What's the big idea? I'm neutral.

OLIVER [*severely shaken*]. That old man looks real, Titmuss—if I can trust my eyes. But can I?

TITMUSS [*dazed*]. I don't know if I'm awake or dreaming. Touch him, and see.

SEXTON. All these here flags must be got up on them trees, they must. But I'll let you in directly; you'll be the first ones of all.

POTTER [*bewildered*]. But there are people inside already. Didn't you hear them? Just as you came.

SEXTON. Bother that boy, he should be here now with the ladder.

POTTER [*louder*]. Are you deaf? I said a whole crowd just went inside.

SEXTON. Eh, sir? No, I don't take no notice of they, not me. Always up to their pranks, specially on the Birthday. Never mind, I'll open up for you now. [*At door.*] Why, he's left the key in the lock.

TITMUSS. Please don't bother. Very kind of you, but we're just going.

OLIVER. But where's Marian?

POTTER. Don't ask me.

OLIVER [*to* BERT]. Have you seen her? Where can she have got to?

BERT. Search me! She was here a minute ago.

POTTER [*picking up rucksack*]. Well, I'm not hanging about. I'm getting out of here. Had enough.

SEXTON. I've seen lots hurry to get here on the Birthday, but none like you, leaving before it starts, as you might say. There's more crowded and crammed here than you could count, later on. For it's St George's Day too. They call him St George of England —dunno where he came from, but William Shakespeare, he were a Stratford man.

OLIVER [*calling*]. Marian! Where are you?

SEXTON [*to himself*]. Funny thing finding the key—it weren't there last night, I'll be sworn. [*A bicycle-bell tinkles, off.*] Ah, that's my boy at last, the lazy lout. And without the ladder, I'll be bound. [*Moving off, scolding.*] Late again, you slug-a-bed. How am I to get the flags up without the ladder? For all the use you are, you might as well not be here.

[OLIVER *looks after him, then round to the church. The clock strikes five.*

OLIVER. There's something rather strange about all this. [*Pause.*] And Marian doesn't answer.

BERT. Shall I go and look?

POTTER. Listen, Albert, you can search for the girl if you like, but I'm not staying in this place, not me. [*He goes off.*

OLIVER. It doesn't seem right to leave her here.

TITMUSS. Don't trouble yourself about her; she's gone. Oh, dear me, yes. Gone. [*Pause.*

BERT. If you say so, I might as well push off, then. [*He picks up cases.*] So long. [*To himself.*] Birds! Lumbered again!

[*He goes off.*

[OLIVER, *still uncertain, takes a last look round. He sees the crowbars and camera on the steps.*

OLIVER. Oh, we'd better take our things. [*He picks them up.*

TITMUSS. They haven't been much use to us, have they? A most frustrating experience; everything seemed to go wrong. Well, we might try again—next year.

OLIVER. You know, I don't think somehow that I will.

[*They go off. The thrush sings.* MARIAN *enters with her coat over her arm and carrying a bunch of wild flowers. She goes down on one knee and lays them in front of the door, then rises, and turns to address the audience.*

MARIAN. If you admit that two wrongs cannot make a right, you will agree that three rights cannot make a wrong—for there is only one right. If Bacon, Oxford, and Marlowe are right, then Shakespeare must be wrong, and that is to wrong Shakespeare. Now those who attempt this may make what mysteries they can, but let them be warned that if they carry the war into his parish they do so at their peril. For if Blackfriars and Bankside are no longer suburbs of Bohemia, Stratford, in fancy, may still border on the Forest of Arden; and if these be all sleeping parishioners under the church tower, there are ever-wakeful guardians keeping watch against invaders—I mean, the actors. For Shakespeare was first an actor, and it is for us actors to take his part, who wrote so many good parts for us; and we stand prepared to employ all the arts of illusion to destroy the enemy's morale and send him packing. That is to say—with the moon. [*A moon-spot comes up.*] The owl, hooting at the moon. [BURBAGE *enters* L.,

H

with owl. Hooting, off.] The dog barking at the owl. [KEMPE *enters* R., *with dog. Barks, off.*] The clock tolling the hour. [CONDELL *enters* L., *with gong, which he strikes.*] The lantern shining in the dark. [SEXTON *enters* R., *with lantern.*] The thrush heralding sunrise. [HEMYNGE *enters* L., *with thrush in cage. Birdsong off as the lights slowly fade up.*

If we offend any here, we ask pardon; if we please some, we thank you for your indulgence; and, taking our leave, make curtsey, and remain your most humble, obedient servants.

[*She curtsies, the men bow.*

The CURTAIN *falls.*

Report from Contreros

By Michael Dines

CHARACTERS

(in the order of their appearance)

CAPTAIN GOMEZ
SERGEANT LUIS
INSPECTOR DIAZ
SENORITA PIDAL
MARIA

The action of the play passes in a small police-station in Spain.

TIME: *The present.*

© 1962 *by Michael Dines*
All Rights Reserved

Applications regarding amateur performances of this play should be addressed to Messrs Samuel French, Ltd, 26 Southampton Street, Strand, London, W.C.2, or Samuel French Inc., 25 West 45th Street, New York.

Report from Contreros

Author's Note

The conflict between the Inspector and Captain is intended to be one between a modern, cultured customs officer and the local, stupid Chief of Police. The play hinges on the fact that this local policeman is far from stupid.

The authentic uniforms of the two policemen, Captain Gomez and Sergeant Luis, consist of jackets and trousers of heavy, blue serge type of material. The Sergeant's jacket will have the usual sergeant's three stripes on the arm while the Captain will have a number of gold stars or dots on the shoulders. As these uniforms, specially the trousers, are naturally baggy, they will form a contrast with the Inspector's better fitting uniform of khaki drill jacket and trousers.

The Inspector will also wear a Sam-Browne type of gun-belt with pistol. The Inspector's cap is a military brown one with peak. The two policemen can be bareheaded or wear peaked caps with white crowns and blue peaks.

Captain Gomez has a heavy moustache. The women wear peasant dress. Maria, as a married woman, will wear more staid clothing than Senorita Pidal.

A plaster cast of the Madonna is used. This is easily obtained but if not, any plaster reproduction could be substituted. If possible the figurine should be broken by the Captain when he discovers the diamonds and again when he tests a small piece for taste. If this is not practical he can find the diamonds inside the hollow figure and later rub some off on to his finger when he identifies its composition.

The Spanish version of the word 'Captain' is given. Either this or the English pronunciation can be used, but if the former, then the Spanish pronunciation of the other terms must also be used. 'Inspector' must be pronounced with the accent on the last syllable, and the name of Diaz as 'Dee-ath.'

SCENE : *The private office of* CAPTAIN GOMEZ, *Chief of Police in the small frontier village of Contreros, in Spain. There is a window* C. *of the back wall and a door to the main office* L. *There is a table down* R. *with chairs* R. *and* L. *of it; on the table are a half-finished game of chess, an assortment of papers and writing equipment, and a hand bell. On the wall behind this table hangs a gunbelt with pistol and holster.* L. *of the windows is a small table on which stand bottles and glasses.* R. *of the window stands a filing cabinet. There are upright chairs down* L. *and* R. *of the drinks table.*

When the curtain rises the sun shines through the window and it is hot. CAPTAIN GOMEZ *is sitting* R. *of the table with his feet stretched out on it or in some equally inelegant position. His jacket is unbuttoned, and he is mopping his face with a large handkerchief because of the heat; at all times all the actors must react to this heat. There is a sound of a car stopping outside. The* CAPTAIN *shouts to the main office.*

CAPTAIN. Luis!

[*The door opens, and* LUIS, *a police sergeant, enters.*
LUIS. Yes, Capitan?
CAPTAIN. A car's just stopped outside. It is most probably the Inspector from the city.
LUIS. Yes, Capitan!
CAPTAIN. Remember what I told you; he will report back to headquarters, and if there is a bad report of the men here, well [*sardonically*], the men will not be here much longer.
LUIS. I understand, Capitan.
CAPTAIN. I hope you do. Tell the others to be most careful.
LUIS. Yes, Capitan.
CAPTAIN. Now! The girl?
LUIS. Maria is with her. She will not be long.

CAPTAIN. Good, Bring her in as soon as she has been searched.
[LUIS *nods.*
Now show the Inspector in.
> [LUIS *nods again and leaves. The* CAPTAIN *waits for his visitor. He moves his legs from the table, buttons up his tunic, puts his handkerchief away, and assumes a business-like manner to impress the Inspector. He straightens a few papers on his desk. There is a knock on the door.*

Come in! [*The door opens and* LUIS *stands in the doorway.*

LUIS. Inspector Rodrigues Diaz of the Customs and Excise is here, Capitan!

CAPTAIN. Ah, good. I will see him!

LUIS. Yes, sir!

[LUIS *exits. He returns at once with* INSPECTOR DIAZ.

CAPTAIN [*rising from his chair, shakes hands with the Inspector*]. Welcome to Contreros, Inspector. [LUIS *exits.*

INSPECTOR. A pleasure to meet you, Capitan Gomez.

CAPTAIN [*gesturing to the chair*]. Please sit down!

INSPECTOR. Thank you. [*He sits* L. *of the table.*] Ah, that's better. [*He stretches.*] The journey was most tiring. [*He relaxes.*] Well, Capitan, you received my message? Everything under control?

CAPTAIN. We carried out your instructions. Everything has been taken care of. [*He moves up* L. *to the bottles.*] But first—a drink, Inspector?

INSPECTOR [*gratefully*]. Please, Capitan. Something long and cold. It is so hot!

CAPTAIN [*pouring drinks*]. We have little crime here. [*He smiles.*] It is rumoured that the reason for this is because the Devil himself cannot stand the heat at Contreros.

> [*He hands the* INSPECTOR *a drink and places the wine bottle on the table.*

INSPECTOR [*taking the drink; he smiles*]. That I can truly believe. [*They drink.*

CAPTAIN. It is a local wine, Inspector. Contreros is justly proud of it as the worst wine in the country. Long and cold are its only virtues.

INSPECTOR. It is most welcome.
CAPTAIN. You are being polite.
[*He sits behind the table again. They drink.*]
INSPECTOR [*reflectively*]. My last assignment was at Narass...
CAPTAIN [*appreciatively*]. Ah! The coast...
INSPECTOR [*dreamily*]. The sea was so blue, the air like perfume. [*He sighs.*] Yes, I left with regret.
CAPTAIN [*laughing*]. But any place is better than Contreros, eh?
[*The* INSPECTOR *smiles tactfully. They drink.*]
INSPECTOR. It is one of the disadvantages of being a customs' officer in a country with a long coastline and an equally long frontier—[*he smiles wryly*] but we do as we're told—not as we wish. [*He puts down the glass for a moment.*] Now, Capitan, I don't want to—er—rush you—but...
CAPTAIN [*gesturing*]. Don't worry, Inspector. Enjoy your drink and relax. As I said, everything is being attended to. The bus arrived ten minutes ago. The girl and her luggage were taken off quietly and without attracting attention and she is now being searched most thoroughly. When this is finished she will be brought in to us.
INSPECTOR [*showing relief*]. Good, good!
CAPTAIN. The search is being made by a woman from the village. She has done this many times and is most expert. I assure you if the girl has one hair out of place—our Maria will find it.
[*He laughs uproariously at his joke.*]
INSPECTOR. Excellent! I shall mention your efficiency to my superiors. [*He pauses; in a friendly tone.*] I hope I am not being too officious?
CAPTAIN [*expansively*]. Not at all, Inspector. After all—one cannot be too careful. A little country police-station—used to handling the odd drunk—the odd theft. [*He gestures.*] To rely on them!
INSPECTOR [*sharply*]. I didn't say that, Capitan!
CAPTAIN [*drinking; smilingly*]. Perhaps not, Inspector. But so many think it.
INSPECTOR [*more gently*]. Number me amongst the exceptions, Capitan!
CAPTAIN. Thank you! And in return may I say how honoured we are at the visit of the redoubtable Inspector Diaz?

INSPECTOR [*bending his head at the compliment*]. You flatter me, Capitan. [*He drinks*]. It may seem a small matter to bring me down here—an ignorant peasant girl suspected of smuggling —but we feel she can lead us to more important people.

CAPTAIN. I gathered that.

INSPECTOR. And it had to be done here. Contreros is the last stop before the highway.

CAPTAIN [*thoughtfully*]. I see. I was wondering about that. [*Amiably.*] Don't misunderstand me, Inspector. We are delighted to co-operate. [*He refills the glasses; laughing.*] In fact, I have always felt that if more of our superiors were to visit the smaller local police-stations they would appreciate our difficulties. [*Still laughing.*] No offence intended, Inspector.

INSPECTOR [*laughing back*]. And none taken, Capitan.

CAPTAIN [*sincerely*]. It is well known in the police service that the renowned Inspector Diaz does not earn his salary by giving orders from a comfortable office in headquarters.

INSPECTOR [*wryly*]. Since I was transferred to the Department of Customs and Excise I think I've seen the inside of every police-station and customs office in the country.

CAPTAIN [*laughing*]. And now Contreros?

INSPECTOR [*in similar mood*]. And now Contreros. [*He drinks.*] There are times when I wish I were back at the easier task of normal police duties.

CAPTAIN [*sympathetically*]. The smuggling keeps you busy?

INSPECTOR. Busy! Whatever we do—it's like a drop in the ocean. We catch one here—one there, and three others take the place of each one. [*He pauses thoughtfully.*] But this latest outbreak is no ordinary increase in smuggling. Too well planned!

CAPTAIN [*nodding in agreement*]. I have seen the report.

INSPECTOR. The Government are concerned. Smuggling on this scale can have serious repercussions. The department of Customs and Excise is also disturbed. Unless something is done—we are afraid many heads will roll. [*Moodily.*] There's so little we can do. We haven't even got enough men as it is.

CAPTAIN [*sighing*]. It is a large country. Many entrances—many exits.

INSPECTOR. I'm afraid so. [*He drinks moodily and both remain lost in gloomy thought for a few moments, then he looks at the door.*] The girl. Will they be much longer?

CAPTAIN [*soothingly*]. In good time. I told you they would be thorough.

INSPECTOR. Of course. [*He drinks.*] I am sorry if I appear impatient. This may be the opportunity we have waited for. If only this girl will reveal anything in interrogation—any clue—any lead—[*he bangs the table with a clenched fist for emphasis*] we could do something!

CAPTAIN [*curiously*]. The report does not say what we are looking for?

INSPECTOR. We don't know that. Anything worth smuggling. Valuable stones—gold—drugs—[*he shrugs*] anything of value and easily converted into currency...

CAPTAIN. What made you first suspect this particular carrier? After all—one peasant girl in so many...

INSPECTOR [*moodily*]. I wish I could say the department had uncovered something. [*He sighs.*] No! An informer!

CAPTAIN [*disgustedly*]. I thought so!

INSPECTOR [*wryly*]. Without them—our job would be hopeless. But always there is the one—[*he shrugs*] for money...

CAPTAIN. Another point that puzzles us. Why have the girl brought here? To a police-station? The bus stopped at Andremo on the border. Surely the customs there could have handled it?

INSPECTOR [*moodily*]. That's one point we're not happy about. It had to be done, though. Up to now all we've managed to catch were a few of the smaller fish, and they've never led us to the important ones. [*Hesitantly.*] It was decided—there was—a possibility—of a leak—in the organization—some one giving information away——

CAPTAIN [*thoughtfully*]. I see...

INSPECTOR. —and that the next carrier to be caught—should be away from the customs office. [*He smiles wryly.*] We chose your station, Capitan. The girl was allowed to go through the Customs without interference.

CAPTAIN. Again I am honoured, Inspector.

INSPECTOR. If anything does come of this—it would be in your favour, Capitan.

CAPTAIN. After eighteen years as Chief of Police in Contreros—I'm afraid my ambition does not aim much higher.

INSPECTOR [*shrugging*]. Who knows—sometimes—events—people... [*He is interrupted by a knock at the door.*

CAPTAIN. Excuse me. [*He shouts.*] Come in.

[*The door opens and* LUIS, *carrying a suitcase, enters with the peasant girl,* SENORITA PIDAL, *and the woman from the village,* MARIA.

CAPTAIN. Ah, Luis, good!

LUIS [*coming over to the table*]. We have brought the girl and her luggage as instructed, Capitan! Her passport!

[*He holds the passport out.*

CAPTAIN [*taking the passport*]. She has been searched?

MARIA [*stepping forward*]. Yes, Capitan!

CAPTAIN. Did you find anything on her?

MARIA [*shaking her head*]. No!

CAPTAIN. You are sure?

MARIA. I am sure.

CAPTAIN [*thoughtfully*]. Um! I see. [*He pauses.*] And the suitcase?

LUIS. As instructed, we left that untouched.

[*The* CAPTAIN *looks to the* INSPECTOR *for guidance.*
[*The* INSPECTOR *waves to him to continue.*

CAPTAIN [*to* SENORITA PIDAL]. Senorita [*looking in the passport*] Pidal! We have information that leads us to believe you are carrying smuggled goods. Have you anything to say?

[SENORITA PIDAL *looks dumbly at the* CAPTAIN.
This can be a serious matter—but if you help us...

[SENORITA PIDAL *continues to look dumbly at the* CAPTAIN. *She is obviously concentrating and trying to understand him.*

[*Gently.*] Senorita, do you understand what I am saying?

[SENORITA PIDAL *nods hesitantly.*

LUIS [*hesitantly*]. Capitan?

[*The* CAPTAIN *looks at* LUIS *inquiringly.*
The girl—she is a little—er... [*He taps his head significantly.*

CAPTAIN [*slowly*]. Yes, I can see that...

MARIA. Since birth—she has been—simple.

CAPTAIN [*to* LUIS]. Where was she going on the bus?
LUIS. To her parents. In Arroga.
CAPTAIN [*to the* INSPECTOR]. A village about thirty kilometres away...
LUIS. She's a kitchen-maid at one of the big houses across the frontier. Twice a year she visits her people.
CAPTAIN [*to* LUIS]. Any record of her having been in any trouble, before?

[LUIS *shakes his head.*]

Well! [*He sighs.*] Let's examine the suitcase.

[*He waves* LUIS *to put the case on the table, then looks at the* INSPECTOR.

INSPECTOR [*rising*]. Please carry on, Capitan.
CAPTAIN [*to* LUIS]. Open it!

[LUIS *opens the case and throws the lid back. The* CAPTAIN *slowly empties the case of its contents, examining each article as he takes it out of the case and puts it on the table. The* INSPECTOR *stands by watchfully but does not interfere. In the case there are various garments, a dress, a skirt, a shawl, some handkerchiefs, etc., a pair of shoes, and a plaster reproduction of the Madonna. The* CAPTAIN *takes out the garments first. He examines each one for concealed objects but finds none. He takes out the pair of shoes and examines them more closely.*

INSPECTOR. False heels?

[*The* CAPTAIN *examines them again, checking the heels and inside the shoes. He shakes his head, and passes them over to the* INSPECTOR *for checking. The* INSPECTOR *takes them, and examines them.*

Nothing there. [*He places the shoes with the other articles.*

[*The* CAPTAIN *takes the last article out of the case, the Madonna. He looks at it doubtfully, shakes his head thoughtfully in concentration. He feels inside and tenses. All in the room show marked interest, the* INSPECTOR *coming closer.*

[*Excitedly.*] You've found something?

[*The* CAPTAIN *takes a little wrapped package from the plaster figurine. He unwraps it, and rolls a few dia-*

> monds on to his open hand. *The* CAPTAIN *and* INSPECTOR *stand looking at the stones.*

[*Exultantly.*] You found it—diamonds!

CAPTAIN [*slowly and thoughtfully*]. Yes, I found it. [*He turns to the girl, showing her the diamonds on his palm.*] What do you know of this, Senorita?

PIDAL [*hesitantly*]. I know nothing. I never see them before.

CAPTAIN. The Madonna is yours?

PIDAL [*shaking her head, in puzzled concentration*]. It belongs to the—man...

INSPECTOR [*quickly*]. What man?

PIDAL. The man—who gave me—the Madonna...

> [*The* INSPECTOR *looks wearily at the* CAPTAIN.

CAPTAIN [*slowly and gently*]. This man? What did he tell you?

PIDAL. I take the—Madonna for him. He give me—money...

CAPTAIN. Where were you supposed to take the Madonna?

PIDAL [*vaguely*]. I don't know. He tells me—I take the Madonna—he will come—for it...

INSPECTOR [*to the* CAPTAIN]. They wouldn't leave any traces. Probably pick up the Madonna at their own time—when they think it's safe.

CAPTAIN [*nodding towards* PIDAL]. We won't get much more out of her.

INSPECTOR. No, I don't think so. We'll try again at headquarters.

CAPTAIN [*to* LUIS]. Lock her up for the time being.

> [LUIS *grasps* PIDAL *by the arm.*

[*To* MARIA.] Thank you, Senorita.

> [MARIA *nods, and, together with* LUIS *and* PIDAL, *prepares to leave.*

[*To* LUIS.] See that she gets some food. She must be starved after that bus journey.

LUIS. Yes, Capitan.   [MARIA, LUIS, *and* PIDAL *exit.*

CAPTAIN [*bitterly*]. They don't care who they use. [*He walks over to the drinks.*] I need a drink. Something stronger. [*He looks at the* INSPECTOR.] Brandy?

> [*The* INSPECTOR *nods. The* CAPTAIN *pours two drinks, and hands one to the* INSPECTOR.

INSPECTOR. My compliments, Capitan, on your efficient handling of the matter. [*He sits in front of the table again.*]
CAPTAIN [*drinking; moodily*]. There was much to handle?
INSPECTOR. That was not your fault. [*He holds his glass up.*] Your health, Capitan Gomez!
[*The* CAPTAIN, *lost in moody thought, nods absent-mindedly in reply to the toast. They drink.*]
CAPTAIN [*moodily*]. You won't do any better with her up at headquarters.
INSPECTOR. We know that. But it's mostly routine now. We'll examine the evidence, check up on the girl's background ...
CAPTAIN. What will happen to her?
INSPECTOR. Oh—we'll let her go free—for the present. She'll be followed day and night in the hope that she'll lead us to one of the big ones—[*he shakes his head doubtfully*] but I doubt it ...
CAPTAIN. And then?
INSPECTOR. In either case, later on, she'll be tried and charged. After that—who knows?
CAPTAIN [*thoughtfully*]. I see. And yet she is probably innocent of any real crime.
INSPECTOR. Oh, quite possibly. In fact, I would swear she is.
CAPTAIN [*grimly*]. The things one must do in our profession!
INSPECTOR. Don't concern yourself, Capitan. The girl is our responsibility now.
CAPTAIN. I wasn't thinking only of the girl.
INSPECTOR [*in surprise*]. What *were* you thinking of?
CAPTAIN [*grimly*]. The truth!
INSPECTOR [*looking at the* CAPTAIN *for explanation*]. Ah?
CAPTAIN. The truth, Inspector Diaz! Because if we want justice—we must have truth!
INSPECTOR [*baffled*]. I'm afraid I don't ...
CAPTAIN [*interrupting him*]. Have you ever noticed that the figure of Justice is usually represented by a woman with her eyes blindfolded? [*With ironic amusement.*] This has always amused me. Justice—which can have only one logical answer! The truth! Depicted by one of God's most illogical creations—a woman! [*He laughs.*] And to make it all the more difficult—she cannot see!

INSPECTOR [*laughing*]. You're a philosopher, Capitan.

CAPTAIN. As I told you before, Inspector. Nothing ever happens here in Contreros. It has one advantage—it gives you time to think.

INSPECTOR [*smiling*]. You seem to have put your time to good use.

CAPTAIN [*pausing, then going off at a tangent*]. Have you ever played chess, Inspector? [*He looks at the chess-board.*]

INSPECTOR [*laughing*]. It is impossible to follow your trend of thought, my dear Capitan. But I do play chess. Many times. It is a game I enjoy.

CAPTAIN. Then perhaps you will appreciate that often in chess, the outcome is unimportant?——

INSPECTOR [*puzzled*]. I don't understand.

CAPTAIN. —but the moves leading up to the result are afterwards discussed and pondered over...

INSPECTOR [*nodding*]. That is true.

CAPTAIN [*almost dreamily*]. Each move at the time—seemingly so illogical in itself—all falling into place at the end of the game...

INSPECTOR. Um, I suppose so...

CAPTAIN. I often associate events with the moves in chess. For example, take those leading up to the affair with this poor peasant girl.

INSPECTOR. I don't see the connexion...

CAPTAIN [*coming closer for emphasis*]. Inspector! Didn't you ever ask yourself why an international smuggling ring, you admitted yourself, one of experienced professionals, should choose such a girl to be their carrier, and then choose an area like Contreros for their purpose? From what I am told, the customs officers at the frontier have had nothing worse than a smuggled camera or watch in the past ten years.

INSPECTOR [*shrugging*]. It happens that way.

CAPTAIN. Agreed! It does happen. But logically it should not! And whenever something illogical occurs one must ask the inevitable question! Is this as it appears or is it an illogical occurrence made to appear logical?

INSPECTOR. I do not understand you, Capitan.

CAPTAIN [*laughing*]. My apologies, Inspector! I do not express myself eloquently. [*Sardonically.*] After all—a rural Chief of Police does not usually have occasion for expressing himself.

INSPECTOR [*lightly*]. I cannot agree with your poor opinion of yourself. At headquarters you are held in much esteem.

CAPTAIN [*wryly*]. Perhaps so. To catch a thief—the odd drunk, and Capitan Gomez is efficient enough!

INSPECTOR [*shrugging*]. A man can only do his job?

CAPTAIN. Agreed!

INSPECTOR. My dear Capitan—where is this conversation leading us?

CAPTAIN. To our unfortunate prisoner. A peasant girl! Half stupid, and incoherent. Knowing nothing of the crime she will go to prison for. [*He pauses.*] Again I ask, why should an experienced ring of smugglers choose such a carrier—a girl who couldn't speak in her own defence if she was caught—*unless* it was *intended* she be caught—[*with irony*] in which case it was suited she couldn't speak?

INSPECTOR [*smiling*]. But surely—it is *most* illogical that a professional smuggling ring should *arrange* for one of its carriers to be caught. [*He laughs.*] There is no profit in *that*!

CAPTAIN [*smiling back*]. On the surface—no! But remember our game of chess? All the illogical moves forming a pattern to a logical end.

INSPECTOR [*rising from his chair*]. I still do not understand these meanderings, Capitan!

CAPTAIN [*shrugging gently*]. I apologize, Inspector! They tell me I talk too much.

INSPECTOR. That may be, but I cannot spend any more time listening to you.   [*He waits for an answer from* GOMEZ.

[*The* CAPTAIN *regards him steadily without answering. For a moment he is disconcerted.*] I thank you for your co-operation and hospitality, and now I must return to headquarters.

[*He moves towards the evidence.*

CAPTAIN [*rising and speaking for the first time directly and with harshness*]. With the evidence, Inspector?

[*The two men are now on opposite sides of the table. At*

this stage the menace in the conversation is apparent, each man now suspicious of the other.

INSPECTOR [*harshly*]. But of course, Capitan!

CAPTAIN [*flatly*]. No!

INSPECTOR [*violently*]. You refuse to obey my orders?

CAPTAIN [*steadily*]. I refuse.

INSPECTOR. I have authority. You will be given an official receipt. Do you think I'll run off with the diamonds?

CAPTAIN. No! The diamonds are safe! I am sure of that!

INSPECTOR. Then what is bothering you?

CAPTAIN. Some outmoded principles such as Justice—Truth, and the answers to some questions!

INSPECTOR [*violently*]. What questions?

CAPTAIN [*vehemently*]. I've already discussed them. Why choose a stupid peasant girl? Why choose Contreros? Why this police-station, and why should a high-ranking inspector attend in person to a task any subordinate could safely do?

INSPECTOR. You think I can answer these questions?

CAPTAIN [*more mildly*]. We shall see—if you will bear with me a little longer, Inspector? [*Dreamily.*] Let us assume that this highly organized and experienced ring of smugglers have an—an —associate in the Department of Customs and Excise. You yourself admitted the possibility of this——

INSPECTOR [*grudgingly*]. It is possible...

CAPTAIN. —and with this advantage our—friends—would be more than stupid to take any chance...

INSPECTOR [*harshly*]. They must always leave something to chance...

CAPTAIN. Only on being caught—or being betrayed...

INSPECTOR. I'm not a fool, I know that!

CAPTAIN [*steadily*]. Then why not eliminate all other possibilities by *allowing* the carrier to be caught?

INSPECTOR. You're talking like an idiot! You don't make sense!

CAPTAIN [*with authority*]. Don't I, Inspector?

[*There is a pause. The* INSPECTOR *tenses but does not answer.* [*Speaking with emphasis.*] I repeat! Let the unsuspecting carrier be caught with something of reasonable value! Say, a few diamonds! The bait is taken, and the real objective is ignored.

[*He picks up the Madonna.*] Something of high value, something easily disposed of—such as drugs. [*He breaks a piece off the Madonna, and, putting it on his tongue, slowly savours it.*] I would say ... Heroin!

[*Slowly and thoughtfully the* INSPECTOR *sits down again.* It would be easy for this organization to find a chemist—[*he contemptuously crumbles a piece of the Madonna*] to mix the drug with chalk and plaster and form it into a figure—later on extracting the drug. [*With contempt.*] And if some of the chalk remains in the drug—who is to complain?

[*The* INSPECTOR *stares down at the table. The* CAPTAIN *looks out of the window. For a short period both men remain lost in thought.*

[*Turning and facing the* INSPECTOR.] And if this suspected associate in the department happens to be of a high rank—[*accusingly*] perhaps even an—*Inspector*—what could be easier? It should fool any ignorant, rural Chief of Police!

INSPECTOR [*dryly*]. I would say far from ignorant!

CAPTAIN [*admiringly*]. So simple! You collect the evidence! Give a receipt! And somewhere in the chain of events substitute a harmless figure. [*In awe.*] Everybody happy! The drug reaches its destination. The authorities have a prisoner! The stupid local police are satisfied with a few words of praise! Everybody happy! [*With bite.*] Except a poor inarticulate girl who cannot speak in her own defence! [*Sarcastically.*] Well! Deny it! Tell me I'm making a mistake!

INSPECTOR [*slowly*]. No mistakes, Capitan!

CAPTAIN. Why did you have to drag an innocent girl into it?

INSPECTOR [*slowly*]. The information from the informer had already reached the department. It had to be acted on.

CAPTAIN. So she was the sacrifice!   [*He turns away in disgust.*

INSPECTOR [*slowly*]. When did you first suspect?

CAPTAIN [*shrugging*]. Who knows? The girl! The diamonds! You! At first a little doubt—a little suspicion, then the certainty!

INSPECTOR. You play a good game of chess, Capitan!

CAPTAIN [*sweeping the chessmen off the table with a violent, angry gesture*]. Not with people as pawns! [*He walks away from the* INSPECTOR.] And I don't like those who traffic in drugs!

I

INSPECTOR. Don't be so high and mighty, Capitan! Not on the pittance they pay us!

CAPTAIN [*sardonically*]. I'm a poor but honest man. [*Wryly.*] The two often go together.

INSPECTOR [*bluntly*]. How much do you earn a week, Capitan?

CAPTAIN [*sardonically*]. Not enough! Our benevolent Government evidently feels that the position of a police officer is sufficient glory in itself.

INSPECTOR. There are some important people in the organization. They can always use a good man. One word from me and you'll live like a lord. For now—a year's salary—and you know nothing!

CAPTAIN. No!

INSPECTOR. I'll double it!

CAPTAIN. No!

INSPECTOR [*violently*]. You're mad! You don't know what you're refusing!

CAPTAIN [*sardonically*]. Don't misunderstand me, my dear Inspector. I am far from incorruptible. If you had suggested this in the first place—before all the pantomime—I might have been interested.

INSPECTOR. Then why not now?

CAPTAIN [*with anger, putting his two hands on the table and glaring across at the* INSPECTOR]. Because your original scheme was based on the principle that Capitan Gomez of the Contreros police-force was a fool who could be easily tricked. [*Sardonically.*] I don't value my integrity so highly but I *do* value my reputation.

INSPECTOR. It would be your word against mine.

CAPTAIN [*picking up the Madonna*]. With that?

[*The* INSPECTOR *stands thoughtfully for a moment. He looks at the* CAPTAIN *and sees his only danger. His hand strays to his holster.*]

[*Grimly.*] I wouldn't! Not with three police officers in the other room.

INSPECTOR. Capitan...

CAPTAIN [*harshly*]. You're finished, Diaz!

INSPECTOR. What are you going to do?

CAPTAIN. Arrest you! For smuggling! [*With venom.*] And I hope they put you away for life...
INSPECTOR. Please, Capitan...
CAPTAIN. One man like you discredits the whole service!
INSPECTOR [*in a low voice*]. I make no excuses, Capitan, but for twenty years I was faithful to a service that demanded everything and paid barely enough to live on...
CAPTAIN [*violently*]. I would rather starve—[*he looks at the Madonna*] than that!
INSPECTOR [*equally violently*]. Do you think I did it for myself? Have you watched your wife go shabbier, do with less, each year, trying to bring up a family? Have you ever watched your wife go old before her time and have to stand by helpless?
CAPTAIN [*steadily*]. I have!
INSPECTOR [*sadly and slowly*]. And then the temptation—and before you know where you are... [*He grasps the* CAPTAIN's *arm.*] Please, Capitan...
CAPTAIN [*with harsh feeling, shrugging him off*]. Don't beg!
INSPECTOR [*steadily*]. I do not beg for myself. I'll resign! I'll do anything you say!
CAPTAIN. It's too late for that.　　　[*He presses the table-bell.*
INSPECTOR [*softly*]. I will not face a trial, Capitan!

[LUIS *enters.*

LUIS. Capitan?
CAPTAIN [*tonelessly*]. You will place Inspector Diaz under arrest!
LUIS [*shocked*]. Ah?
CAPTAIN [*harshly*]. You heard me! Place the Inspector under arrest!

[LUIS *moves towards the* INSPECTOR. *He places his hand tentatively on the* INSPECTOR's *shoulder. The* INSPECTOR *shrugs it off.*

INSPECTOR [*slowly*]. One favour, Capitan?
CAPTAIN [*coldly*]. You deserve none!
INSPECTOR. If not for myself—for the service!

[*The* CAPTAIN *looks steadily at the* INSPECTOR *who looks back at him unwaveringly.*

CAPTAIN. What is it?

INSPECTOR. I have some papers in the car. [*He pauses.*] They explain everything. [*Slowly.*] May I get them?

LUIS [*moving towards the door*]. I'll get them, Capitan!

CAPTAIN [*thoughtfully—without taking his eyes off the* INSPECTOR]. No. Stay where you are. [*To the* INSPECTOR.] Get them!

[*The* INSPECTOR *walks slowly and silently out. He stops at the doorway, and looks back at the* CAPTAIN *in unspoken gratitude.*

INSPECTOR [*softly*]. Thank you. [*The* INSPECTOR *goes out.*]

LUIS [*puzzled*]. But, Capitan! He will—run away...

CAPTAIN [*sitting wearily down*]. Don't interfere. He will not run away. [*Sadly.*] He has nowhere to run to.

[*He rests his head on his arms. He appears very tired and weary.*

[LUIS *stands by patiently.*

[*He points to the bottle.*] Pour me a drink. Take one yourself.

[LUIS *pours two drinks, gives the* CAPTAIN *one. They both take a sip at their drinks when there is the sound of a pistol shot off-stage, followed by excited voices and the sound of running footsteps.* LUIS *moves to the window and looks out. The* CAPTAIN *shows no emotion.*

LUIS [*agitated*]. Capitan—he's—he's...

[*He looks at the* CAPTAIN *uncomprehendingly.*
[*The* CAPTAIN *returns his gaze silently.* LUIS *lets his hands fall to his side in understanding and resignation.*

CAPTAIN [*steadily*]. Inform headquarters that we have arrested the carrier as instructed. Also that we have further information from an unknown source concerning the smuggling ring. Also, we regret to report an accident. As Inspector Diaz was cleaning his pistol, an unfortunate accident occurred. We are sending a report from Contreros...

As the CAPTAIN *is talking—*

the CURTAIN *falls.*

Trouble on Helicon

By Bryan Stocks

© *Bryan Stocks* 1965

CHARACTERS

(in the order of their appearance)

Chorus, *a young girl*
Comatas, *a goatherd*
Calliope, *muse of Epic Poetry*
Clio, *muse of History*
Erato, *muse of Love Poetry*
Euterpe, *muse of Lyric Poetry*
Polyhymnia, *muse of Lyric Poetry and Eloquence*
Melpomene, *muse of Tragedy*
Terpsichore, *muse of the Dance*
Thalia, *muse of Comedy*
Urania, *muse of Astronomy*
Polixenes, *a herdsman and farmer*
The Voice of Zeus

Applications regarding amateur performances of this play should be addressed to Messrs Samuel French, Ltd, 26 Southampton Street, Strand, London, W.C.2, or Samuel French Inc., 25 West 45th Street, New York.

Trouble on Helicon

SCENE: *Mount Helicon, beside the Fountain of Hippocrene,* C. U.L. *there stands a shrine dedicated to the nine muses,* U.R. *there is the doorway of an old shepherd's hut.* D.R. *there is some shrubbery.*
Enter CHORUS L.

CHORUS [*affably but with a touch of condescension*].
Good evening, mortals. Welcome to our play
"Trouble on Helicon," but before it starts
Allow me words to set the scene for you.
To-night you are in exalted company,
For now you stand upon Mount Helicon,
Where the nine muses have their puissant court,
Direct the world's affairs, and take their sport—
With goddess-like propriety, I add.
In moonlight, on a certain summer's eve,
A shepherd-boy, Comatas, brought his flock
To browse upon this hallowed hill. As night
Came on he scorned to turn to home and bed
But stayed upon Mount Helicon instead.
As the moon rose, he strolled, his pipe in hand,
              [*Enter* D.R. COMATAS. *Soft pipe-music is heard.*
Near to the fountain they call Hippocrene.
So starts our story and begins our scene.
                           [CHORUS. *Exit* L.
COMATAS *looks about him with interest, at the fountain and the shrine, then continues playing his pipe and begins to go on his way. At this moment he hears music not his own, and looks round to know where it comes from* [*Music swells.*] *Seeing figures approaching off* L. *he quickly hides in the shrubbery,* D.R. *but watches with absorbed interest what follows.*

Enter U.L. *the nine muses. They are similarly dressed in classical Greek costume.* CALLIOPE *is laurel-crowned,* CLIO *carries a quill and ink horn at her girdle,* ERATO *carries a lyre,* POLYHYMNIA *carries a sceptre,* THALIA *carries a shepherd's crook and wears a garland. The music ends, and the muses relax and dispose of their respective props. The light fades, and there is a distant roll of thunder. All look up at the sky.*

THALIA [*wearily*]. Oh, dear, what's the matter now?
EUTERPE. It's father again. He's in one of his tempers.
MELPOMENE [*briskly*]. Oh, well! Come along, then!
 [*The muses group themselves about the fountain.* MELPOMENE *signals, and the music is played again. The muses dance a brief ritualistic figure. Music ends. Pause. All look up. Light brightens.*
CLIO. Thank Aphrodite that's over! I sometimes think we carry these rites too far.
URANIA. They are for mortals. We should be above that sort of thing.
TERPSICHORE. How can you say that? Dancing only for mortals? It's far too good for them as it is.   [*Dances a few steps.*
EUTERPE. Yes, we all know how beautifully you do it, Terpsichore.
TERPSICHORE. Oh, but I could have danced all night.
 [CLIO *looks interested, and, taking up her pen and scroll, makes note of the phrase.*
EUTERPE. I believe you could.
MELPOMENE [*dramatically*]. What is there to dance about, I should like to know! Nothing at all! I sometimes wish that *I* were mortal.
TERPSICHORE. Oh, do cheer up, Melpomene—just for a century or so.
MELPOMENE. I will not "cheer up." What a vulgar expression, by the way.
ERATO. I can't understand how anybody can be miserable on a night like this. It's so still, I can hear the crickets down in the forest. And just look at the moon! It is a night made for lovers.

URANIA. I think you'll find that climatic conditions have really very little to do with people's emotions. The mortals cling to that theory, I know, as to many others, but they are wrong, of course. The stars control everything.

CLIO. Yes, just what the historians say, so it must be right.

ERATO. Oh, dear.

CALLIOPE [*enthusiastically*]. It is a night for heroic deeds! I can imagine armies on the march or encamped about a beleaguered city! Can't you hear the tramp of feet and see the moonlight flash on the bare steel as the men unsheath their swords?

THALIA. Very dramatic, dear, but why so bloodthirsty? You remind me of those stupid people who say, "What glorious weather. What shall we kill to-day?"

CALLIOPE. Then what do you suggest?

THALIA. Like every night—it is a night for laughter. Even mortals know that. They toil all day, poor things, because they have to, worrying their heads about crops and money and all sorts of tiresome trivialities. But in the evening they forget everything except that great healing balm of mirth. They sit in taverns and sing, or play games and argue and fight, then make it up and carouse together. Sometimes a few of them put on unusual clothes and perform for the others, and they all laugh immoderately. It is called "amateur theatricals."

MELPOMENE. I am afraid I should not approve of "amateur theatricals."

THALIA. I sometimes wonder, Melpomene, dear, whether you approve of anything.

POLYHYMNIA. Surely you know by now that Melpomene is only really happy when she is miserable. [*To* MELPOMENE.] Never mind, dear. Remember that every silver lining has a cloud.

TERPSICHORE. Do let's dance again.

MELPOMENE. Certainly not. There has been quite enough frivolity for one evening as it is.

CALLIOPE. I do wish I could persuade those lazy Spartans to make war on somebody. It's just the weather for it. Imagine, as the clouds drift across the moon, the assault party creeps forward—slowly, stealthily. [*She does so towards the bush where*

COMATAS *is hiding.* D.R.] Every tree has eyes, and behind every bush there is a—[*comes face to face with* COMATAS *as he peers out between the leaves.* CALLIOPE *jumps back*]—oh! There's somebody there!

POLYHYMNIA. Nonsense! Your imagination is playing you tricks.

CALLIOPE. There is, there is, I tell you. I saw his face just now.

MELPOMENE [*advancing towards the bush*]. I will handle this. You, whoever you are, come out, sir! [*Nothing happens.*] Very well. [*Goes behind the bush,* COMATAS *goes the other way.* MELPOMENE *changes her direction too, and drags him out.*] Now, sir, kindly explain yourself.

COMATAS [*smiling disarmingly*]. Good evening, ladies!

MELPOMENE. Who are you, and what were you doing there?

COMATAS [*quite confidently*]. My name is Comatas, and I'm a goatherd. I'm usually home long before this, but it was such a lovely evening, I decided to stay on the mountain. I must say I'm glad I did.

MELPOMENE. Indeed!

COMATAS. Who are you, by the way?

MELPOMENE [*with heavy irony*]. By the way, I am Melpomene, muse of Tragedy. On your knees, mortal! [COMATAS *kneels.*] That's better.

COMATAS [*timidly now*]. And are all these your sisters? What are their names?

CALLIOPE. I am Calliope, muse of Epic Poetry. I admit I can't be too critical of your behaviour—I was just remarking what a fine night it would be for manœuvres!

COMATAS. I write poetry sometimes.

CALLIOPE [*coldly*]. Indeed?

COMATAS [*gaining confidence*]. I always wanted to be a poet instead of just a goatherd. Do you know, I once wrote a poem in your honour. Shall I recite it?

CALLIOPE. How many lines?

COMATAS. A hundred and sixty-four.

CALLIOPE [*repressing a yawn*]. Thank you—not just now.

CLIO. My name is Clio—history, you know. I get blamed for

nearly everything that's written on the subject, but in point of fact few mortals realize how much I do on their behalf. I spend most of my time trying to persuade professors not to be pedantic and retired generals not to write their memoirs—unfortunately with little success.

TERPSICHORE. I'm Terpsichore—muse of the Dance.

COMATAS. I knew it! How graceful you are, and how beautifully you move.

TERPSICHORE. Thank you—I know.

POLYHYMNIA. I am Polyhymnia, and this my sceptre proclaims that of all arts eloquence is sovereign. Eloquence, that noblest gift of the gods, distinguishes man from the lower animals. It is of all gifts the one he should cherish the most——

THALIA. Yes, dear, and I'm sure he does.

POLYHYMNIA. —for it enables him to invoke the help of all the gods persuasively and to answer them when they call upon him——

CALLIOPE. I think that about covers the subject.

POLYHYMNIA. See to it, therefore, young man, that you practise and venerate this sovereign art of eloquence. Orate as often as possible, and, if nobody will listen, why then soliloquize! In short, keep ever bright this blessed art, and never allow anything or anybody to degrade your burgeoning talent into mere conversation.

COMATAS [*meekly*]. Thank you, I won't.

THALIA. I am not, as you might expect, the muse of Anticlimax! I am the muse of Comedy, and I do wish I could truthfully say that something funny happened to me on my way to Helicon this evening. In point of fact, nothing did—nothing ever does! Funny things, you see, only happen to the serious, like Polyhymnia or Melpomene.

MELPOMENE. Why are they funny when they happen to me?

THALIA. Because tragedy is one's own misfortunes, comedy those of other people.

COMATAS. You make the whole thing very—clear!

THALIA [*tartly*]. I do my best, though lacking the brilliant eloquence of my sister!

COMATAS [*to* URANIA]. And what do you do?

MELPOMENE [*indignantly*]. Is *that* the way to address a *goddess*? Is this some sort of celestial Labour Exchange?

COMATAS. Forgive me, I am not used to meeting immortals.

MELPOMENE. That is quite obvious.

URANIA. I, mortal, am the muse of Astronomy. All you do and all you are depends upon the position of the stars at the moment of your birth. In that hour your destiny is fixed, and all your life will be guided by their influence. Be warned against the false pride of choosing your own path, for you will be punished for it. Seek the guidance of the stars, and defy them not.

COMATAS. Of course not. Thank you. Oh, I do hope I shall be able to remember all this good advice.

MELPOMENE. You must make the most of it. We never grant interviews to mortals as a rule.

ERATO. I think you will have heard of me. I am Erato, muse of the Poetry of Love. [*Advances towards him.*] You probably think —lots of mortals do—that there is nothing new to be said upon this fascinating topic, but that's not true. Do you know, I can cast my spell by merely going up to somebody like this, then making a circle [*encircles* COMATAS] this way, then another circle that way. [*Goes round him the other way.*] The result? The poor man falls hopelessly in love with the very next person he looks at! [*Pause.*

CALLIOPE. Nothing much appears to have happened in this case!

   [COMATAS *sinks to his knees looking rigidly before him. Then very slowly his head turns towards* EUTERPE, *and he gazes fixedly at her.*

COMATAS [*tensely*]. You are Euterpe, and I love you.

MELPOMENE [*aghast*]. What? Erato, just look what you've done.

POLYHYMNIA. Hardly the person she intended, I think!

MELPOMENE. Something like this always happens when protocol is not observed. The interview is over. It should never have taken place. Come, my sisters.

   Turns and leads off L. *Music is heard. The rest follow except* EUTERPE *who stands gazing at* COMATAS. ERATO *holds out her hands towards her helplessly.* EUTERPE *ignores her.* ERATO *looks anxiously after the departed muses, then at* EUTERPE *and* COMATAS. *Finally, apprehensive at what she has done, she runs off to follow the rest. Music fades.*

EUTERPE. You can stand up if you like.

COMATAS. Oh, yes. Thank you. [*Pause.*] I can't think of anything to say.

EUTERPE. You don't have to say anything.

COMATAS. There's something I'd like to do.

EUTERPE [*mockingly*]. Is there? What?

COMATAS. I'd like to burst forth into poetry—sublime poetry, in praise of you!

EUTERPE. It could be arranged but I find silence even more flattering. The deepest feelings are inexpressible.

COMATAS. Yes, of course, you're right. What a lot I'm learning to-day!

MELPOMENE [*off*]. Euterpe! Euterpe!

COMATAS [*nervous but suddenly confidential*]. It was so funny. All your sisters were strangers to me and rather frightening. You I recognized at once, as if I'd known you for years.

EUTERPE [*rather stiffly*]. Really? Tell me, what is it like, this actually being in love?

COMATAS. Well, everything is changed somehow, the whole world and everything in it. In a way, it is through the woman he loves that a man suddenly begins to see life clearly and to understand it.

EUTERPE. And falling out of love?

COMATAS. Terrible! One feels cold and alone, and the lovers just become people again.

EUTERPE. For one so young you clearly know a lot about it.

COMATAS. You're laughing at me.

EUTERPE. Perhaps, a little. Remember, I have heard all the love songs that were ever written. And they're all by men, you know!

COMATAS [*suddenly bold*]. I've noticed that, too. Isn't it surprising how few women can write good poetry—! [*Feels he has gone too far. Kneels down again.*] I'm sorry, I shouldn't have said that!

EUTERPE [*majestically*]. No, you should not! I'm rather an

expert on human emotions. A man's love is often fine, passionate, noble, unselfish, and generous—but it is so rarely durable.

COMATAS. Mine is, I swear it.

EUTERPE [*hastily*]. No, don't. If you were to swear on oath I should have to take note of it in my official capacity, and then, if later you broke it—no, it doesn't bear thinking about!

COMATAS. But my love for you is different, Euterpe.

EUTERPE [*sharply*]. Will you please stop contradicting me! Really, it's as bad as those eternal family gatherings on Mount Parnassus. You will only fall in love with my permission. If and when you do, I shall inform you of the fact. Until then perhaps you will allow me to know better on these matters. We will discuss what you like. From time to time you may differ from me. I will even permit some opposition—but not too much. Let that be clearly understood. Have you anything to say?

COMATAS [*timidly*]. Well—yes! But you won't be pleased.

EUTERPE [*relenting*]. Tell me what it is. I shan't be angry.

COMATAS [*timidly*]. It's nothing much—only that—er—

EUTERPE. Only what?

COMATAS. You can't possibly know *all* about love!

EUTERPE [*angrily*]. Comatas!

COMATAS [*kneeling again*]. I'm sorry, but you insisted. How can you, though, really? Until you've been in love with a mortal it's only theory, isn't it?

EUTERPE [*suddenly pensive*]. There may be something in what you say.

COMATAS [*getting up*]. I would do anything for you, Euterpe. Anything! I would die for you!

EUTERPE [*gently*]. You don't have to do that, Comatas.

COMATAS. I would. I tell you, I would. And I'll prove it. [*He draws his knife.*] I'll show you! I'll show you! [*Rushes off* D.R.

EUTERPE [*desperately*]. No, Comatas! No. Comatas, don't do it! I believe you. [*In horror.*] Oh, what have you done?

COMATAS [*entering* D.P. *carrying a dead kid*]. I've killed a kid! For you, Euterpe!

EUTERPE. Oh, the poor thing!

COMATAS [*goes up to the shrine* U., *erected to the muses, and places the kid upon it, kneeling*]. This sacrifice I offer at the shrine dedicated to the muses, in token of my undying love for Euterpe, goddess of lyric poetry, whom I shall ever love and revere, both in this world and in the next, if circumstances permit. [*Rises.*] There!

EUTERPE [*going to him*]. Oh, Comatas! I believed you all the time!

COMATAS [*ironically*]. My goddess, how like a woman. [*They embrace, there is a long roll of thunder and a flash of lightning.*] Gracious, what's that?

EUTERPE. That, I'm very much afraid, is Father. He usually thunders when he is going to say something, just as a mortal father clears his throat. It means he expects silence.

[*More thunder.*

ZEUS [*off*]. Euterpe, from where he sits on high,
Nothing escapes your father's watchful eye.
Young man, let go her hand! She is divine!
Do you imagine that she could be thine?
Take care you are not punished for your pride
O mortal, seeking an immortal bride!
It shall go hard with you if once my ire
Is roused. There is an everlasting fire
That hungers for the victims of my wrath:
There in the furnace shall you plight your troth!
Now part for ever. Boy, to your home, away!
Daughter, to me! See that you both obey!

[*Roll of thunder.*

COMATAS [*frightened*]. Does that sort of thing often happen?

EUTERPE. Quite often, but he's very sweet really.

COMATAS. It's frightening.

EUTERPE. The first time I suppose it is. You've gone quite pale. Is your undying love as strong as ever?

COMATAS [*uncertainly*]. Yes, yes—of course!

EUTERPE. I'd better go now, or he'll probably start throwing thunderbolts.

COMATAS. When shall I see you again?

EUTERPE. I return here every evening with my sisters. Come at moonrise, and call my name. Good-bye!

[*They kiss, roll of thunder,* EUTERPE *exits hastily* U.L.

COMATAS [*rhapsodically*]. Euterpe!

[*Sighs and turns slowly to exit* R.

POLIXENES [*off* R., *calling*]. Comatas! Comatas! Where is the boy? [*Enters* D.R.] Comatas, here you are. What is the meaning of this? What are you doing here?

COMATAS. Don't be angry, master. Your flocks are safe. The night was warm, and I decided to stay on the mountain.

POLIXENES [*mollified*]. Oh—oh, I see. I was worried about them—and you, of course. What is this place?

COMATAS. The Fountain of Hippocrene, master, and this is a shrine dedicated to the—

[*Stops short as he remembers about the kid.*
[POLIXENES *looks at the shrine up* L.

POLIXENES. And what is this upon it—a sacrifice, eh? [*Furious.*] Why, it's a kid—one of my own flock! Well, what do you say to this, boy?

COMATAS. I offered it on your behalf, master——

POLIXENES. You did, did you? How dare you, without my consent?

COMATAS. It will bring the Muses' protection upon us both.

POLIXENES [*very angrily*]. Will it, indeed? They will be hard put to it to protect you from me. [*Grabs* COMATAS *and drags him, struggling, to a disused shepherd's hut at side of stage,* U.R. *Pushes* COMATAS *in and bangs and locks the door.*] In this shepherd's hut you can meditate on what you have done.

COMATAS [*within*]. Spare me, master.

POLIXENES. No, I will not. I'll teach you a lesson, my boy! Sacrifices to the gods, indeed! Even if a man was stupid enough to believe all that nonsense, wouldn't he take an old goat, one that was tough and dry—instead of a kid?

COMATAS [*within*]. Master! Master!

POLIXENES. You'll cool your heels in there. I'll take the flocks down myself. Sacrifices! [*Exit* D.R.

[*Enter* CHORUS D.L.

CHORUS. Such was the meeting, on Mount Helicon,
Between Euterpe and the shepherd-boy,
Comatas. Though opposed by mighty Zeus
The goddess came again to meet the boy.

She found him not, for old Polixenes
In anger at the lad's love-sacrifice
Had locked him in a disused shepherd's hut
And meant to leave him there. Meanwhile her calls
Echoed across the hillside. No reply
Came to her ears, nor did her mortal love
Appear until one day, in wandering, she
Came near the shepherd's hut—but you shall see!

[*Enter* EUTERPE U.L.
[CHORUS *remains on stage* D.L.

EUTERPE [*calling*]. Comatas! Comatas! [*Advances near the hut, hears her name called softly within.*] What was that? Who's there?

COMATAS [*feebly, within*]. Euterpe.

EUTERPE. Somebody called my name. Comatas, is that you? What has happened?

COMATAS. I am here, Euterpe. My master was angry because I sacrificed a kid, and locked me in here. I am faint with hunger. I shall die and never see you again.

EUTERPE. I have no power to free you. [*Enter* U.L. ERATO *and* THALIA.] Oh, my sisters, help me. Polixenes, master of Comatas, has imprisoned him here, and he is dying of hunger.

ERATO. What was his fault?

EUTERPE. He sacrificed one of his master's flock in my honour!

THALIA. I prophesy they'll say in years to be
This was no treatment for an employee.

EUTERPE. You, dear Erato, made the spell that bound us—tell me, will you see your sister lose her mortal lover?

COMATAS. I am faint. Bring help quickly!

THALIA. Perhaps our cousin Hephaestus could be summoned from his rocky island where the smoke from his forge daily testifies to his interest in metallurgy. For him to break this lock and free Comatas would be simple.

ERATO. Do that—for a *mortal*?

THALIA. No, you are right.

EUTERPE. What can we do?

ERATO. The bees! The bees! Euterpe, do you remember that summer when bees swarmed on Helicon, here near the fountain of Hippocrene?

K

EUTERPE. I do. How can this help my poor Comatas?

ERATO. In solemn conclave, we gave them our consent to stay upon these slopes, taking the pollen from the mountain flowers.

EUTERPE. Dear sister, to the point.

ERATO. Is it so foolish what the mortals say,
That somehow love will always find a way?
Ask—no, command the bees in loyalty to their landlords—that is us—to carry their nectar here, enter this hut by the lock and nourish your unhappy tenant, Comatas!

EUTERPE. Dearest Erato, this moment will I put your plan
                                                to work.

You bees who drain the flowers of Helicon,
And those who drink the honeyed nectar on
Hymettus and on Hybla, hear my plea!
O bring your golden harvest here to me!
Fly to this hut and there, in tiny sips,
Place your sweet load on my beloved's lips!
Now save Comatas with your fragrant store
That he and I may bless you evermore!   [*Pause.*

[*Sound of many bees.*] They're coming! Comatas, help is on the way! Now shall you live and soon be re-united with your Euterpe!

ERATO. Come, sister. We must not linger lest the anger of our father Zeus fall upon us all.

EUTERPE. Why does he deal so severely with me? All the gods know that he himself is not above an occasional amorous——

                                           [*A roll of thunder.*

        [*They all three hurry off* U.L.; *hum of bees continues.*

CHORUS. So was Comatas nourished by the bees
And saved from starving. After many days,
His master came, repenting of his act,
To where Comatas lay within his cell.

                                          [*Enter* POLIXENES D.R.

POLIXENES. The boy must be still in the hut. I'd forgotten all about him. That's what comes of getting into a temper. What shall I do if he's dead? [*Goes to the hut and unlocks it.*] Comatas! Comatas! Are you all right?

COMATAS [*walking briskly out*]. Yes thank you. Didn't I tell you that the Muses would protect me?

POLIXENES [*astonished*]. But this is a miracle! [*Kneels.*] Now do I believe in their power. Don't think too hardly of me, lad. I was in a rage—and all for the sake of one kid. Sacrifice another if you want to, whenever you like.

COMATAS. Thank you! You are pardoned!

POLIXENES [*very much relived*]. No, no, thank *you*!

COMATAS. You'd better go and see to the flocks now. I have more important things to attend to.

POLIXENES. Yes. Yes, of course. Thank you, my boy. I knew you would understand.   [*Exits* D.R. *hastily.*

COMATAS [*calling*]. Euterpe! Where are you?

                              [*Enter* EUTERPE L.

EUTERPE. Oh, dear Comatas—you're free at last! [*They embrace and stroll* U.S., *their arms about each other.*] My Comatas!

COMATAS. Dearest Euterpe! I thought I should never see you again!   [*Exit* U.R.

CHORUS. So ends our story, on this happy scene,
So were the lovers, mortal and immortal,
Re-united. Summer died and autumn came
To Helicon [*leaves fall*], but their love flowered still.

            [*The lovers stroll in* U.R. *and cross stage.*

Euterpe came whenever potent Zeus
Was otherwise engaged—we'll ask not how.

                           [*Lovers re-enter* U.L.

Comatas to his friends' astonishment
Became the finest poet in all Greece.

    [*The lovers cross the stage* U.L. *to* U.R.; *this time* COMATAS *is
        laurel-crowned.*

Lauded and honoured all his happy life!
Only one critic would not give him praise—
Most strange the sudden ending of *his* days
For, as he wrote, he drew his latest breath

                    [*Lovers exit* U.R. *confidentially.*

And rumour has it, he was *stung* to death,
While some suggest, though a harsh thing to say,
All critics should be dealt with in this way.

And so we leave the lovers as they walk
In sweet communion. We do not hear their talk
As they so slowly pace the leaf-strewn grove.
It's tedious—except to those in love!

[Music swells.
[The eight remaining muses enter L., and, going to the fountain, prepare for their rites. Miming, they look about for EUTERPE *and call her, then, deciding to start without her, they do a brief, perfunctory version of their dance. When it is finished they break up, four standing to face audience L., four to face audience R. Enter* POLIXENES *L., and crosses to join group at R.* CHORUS *remains L. Still no sign of* EUTERPE *and* COMATAS. *The rest look about them, desperately calling in mime. Then* MELPOMENE *walks determinedly to the shepherd's hut, throws open the door, and makes a gesture to come out. Enter from hut* EUTERPE *and* COMATAS, *rather abashed, to take up their position at the centre of the company.*

The CURTAIN *falls.*

The Devil's Limelight

By Ella Adkins

© *Ella Adkins* 1965

CHARACTERS

Mrs Marfield
Arthur \} her sons
Stephen /
Jennifer, *her daughter*
Linda, *Stephen's wife*
Miss Pike
Bob Wallace, *a newspaper reporter*
Bill Holland

The action of the play passes in a room in Mrs Marfield's house.

Time: *The present.*

Applications regarding amateur performances of this play should be addressed to Messrs Samuel French, Ltd, 26 Southampton Row, Strand, London, W.C.2, or Samuel French Inc., 25 West 45th Street, New York.

The Devil's Limelight

SCENE I: *A room in Mrs Marfield's house in Barnet, about eleven o'clock on a Saturday morning in early autumn. The room is tastefully but not expensively furnished. Doors* U. R. *and* L.; *french windows* U.C.; *table with drinks, glasses, etc.,* U.R.C.; *writing-table with telephone* D.R.; *settee* D.R.C.; *armchair* D.L.C.; *sideboard or table* U.L. *Other furniture at the discretion of the producer and according to the size of the stage.*

At rise of curtain, JENNIFER, *aged about fifteen, is discovered on settee, reading a newspaper. Enter* LINDA R. *She is a very attractive girl in the early twenties, wearing pyjamas and a dressing-gown. She helps herself to a cigarette, then goes* D.R.C. *to settee and looks over* JENNIFER'S *shoulder.*

LINDA. H'm! Who is she?

JENNIFER. A call-girl witness in the Archer case. Want to read about it?

LINDA [*taking newspaper*]. Quite a dish, isn't she? Hello, I see Lord Dolchester's pegged out at last.

JENNIFER. Who's he?

LINDA. A bit of a ram, from all accounts.   [JENNIFER *giggles.*

[*Enter* MISS PIKE L. *with plate of cake. She is very pleasant-looking, quiet in manner and dress; aged in the sixties.*

JENNIFER. Careful, Linda, or you'll shock Auntie Pie.

MISS PIKE [*placing plate on sideboard*]. There. Apricot flan. Arthur's favourite sweet.

JENNIFER [*to* LINDA]. He's coming to lunch, so you'd better get dressed.

LINDA. Just for my darling brother-in-law? Why? As a doctor, he's probably seen worse.

JENNIFER [*returning to newspaper*]. They say she had real mink on her coat.

LINDA. Who?

JENNIFER. This girl in the case. Gosh! I wish I could wear clothes like that!

MISS PIKE. Your mother would like you to give her a hand with the vegetables.

JENNIFER [*rising reluctantly and going off* L.]. Oh. All right. I'll be glad when I can leave school and have a life of my own.

LINDA. My head feels ghastly. It must be that filthy gin we drank at the Fergusons' last night.

MISS PIKE [*arranging flowers in vase on sideboard*]. Would you like an aspirin?

LINDA. No, thanks. My stomach's like a chemist's shop already.

MISS PIKE. I understand.

LINDA. You don't, my dear, because tea's your tipple.

MISS PIKE. I used to go to parties years ago.

LINDA. I'll bet you did. And you all stood round the piano singing the *Indian Love Lyrics*.

MISS PIKE. We did a lot of silly things in those days.

LINDA. What made you come here, I mean to this house? You're free, no family ties.

MISS PIKE. I think that's why. The children were quite young when I first came, and they never treated me as a lodger. Somehow it's always been like home.

LINDA. It's not my idea of a home, sharing this suburban henhouse with my mother-in-law. Don't you think a married couple should have a place of their own?

MISS PIKE. If possible, yes.

LINDA. I've been trying to make Stephen see that for the past two years.

MISS PIKE. Can't you manage the deposit?

LINDA. Deposit? Oh, yes, and spend the rest of our lives paying off the mortgage. I've seen too much of that.

MISS PIKE. Why not rent a flat?

LINDA. Because Stephen's salary won't run to it. I saw a lovely maisonette the other day in St John's Wood. Twelve guineas a week.

MISS PIKE. You could find something much cheaper.

LINDA. I suppose so; one of those ghastly hovels with the sink on the landing. Oh, if only Stephen would wake up! He can't expect to make money working for a firm that only sells educational stuff. Who wants poetry and highbrow music in these days?

MISS PIKE. He seems to like his job.

LINDA. He'd like anything easy that left him plenty of time for browsing in books. He's absolutely no idea of getting on in life. Sometimes I think he ought to have been a teacher.

MISS PIKE. Still, if he's happy ...

LINDA. He's getting nowhere. You know Jack Carlman?

MISS PIKE. I've heard you speak of him.

LINDA. He came over here a few years ago—a refugee. And look at him now—a posh car, marvellous flat, and everything he wants. If he could do it, surely——

[*Enter* STEPHEN R. *He is a good-looking young man of about twenty-five; a thoughtful, sensitive type. Just now he is looking worried and preoccupied. He is nervous and jumpy throughout the scene.*

MISS PIKE. Good morning, Stephen.

STEPHEN. Good morning.

LINDA. Have you finished in the bathroom?

STEPHEN. Yes.

LINDA. You've been long enough. [*Going off* R.] It's absurd having only one bathroom in a house this size.

STEPHEN [*anxiously*]. Has there been a phone call for me?

MISS PIKE. Not while I've been here.

[STEPHEN *goes to telephone and dials number.*

MISS PIKE. That party must have gone on too long last night. Shall I get you a cup of tea?

STEPHEN. Don't trouble, Auntie Pie, I'll have one later.

MISS PIKE [*going off* L. *with flowers*]. I'll give these fresh water.

STEPHEN [*into phone*]. Hello. Is that Mayfair 0019? Is Mr. Carlman there? ... Do you know what time he'll be in? ... I see. ... Will you ask him to phone Barnet 8410? ... Yes ... It's Stephen Marfield speaking. Yes. ... Thank you.

[*Enter* MRS MARFIELD *with a cup of tea on a small tray.*

MRS MARFIELD. Here you are, Stephen. I've brought you a cup of tea.

STEPHEN [*replacing receiver*]. Thanks, Mother.

MRS MARFIELD. You're not looking well.

STEPHEN. Too many late nights, I expect.

MRS MARFIELD. You're worried. Is anything the matter?

STEPHEN. No, of course not.

MRS MARFIELD. Nothing wrong at work?

STEPHEN. What could go wrong in a dull job like mine?

MRS MARFIELD. I thought you were happy in it.

STEPHEN. I am. At least, I could be.

MRS MARFIELD [*with a sigh*]. It's not easy being a mother-in-law. There's so much I want to say but mustn't.

STEPHEN. Don't worry, Mother. Linda's a grand girl, really. It's just that—well—she's ambitious. We don't always go for the same things.

[*The telephone rings and* STEPHEN *rushes to answer it.*

MRS MARFIELD. You are jumpy this morning.

STEPHEN [*into phone*]. Hello. Barnet 8410. Is that— Who? [*Surprised and disappointed.*] The *Sunday Globe*? ... Yes. ... Yes, there is a Miss Pike living here. ... Yes, I think so. Do you want to speak to her? ... I see. Very well.

[*Rings off.*

That was a reporter from the *Sunday Globe*. Wanted Miss Pike, of all people.

MRS MARFIELD. Why didn't you call her?

STEPHEN. He said he was coming round, and rang off.

MRS MARFIELD. I'd better let her know.

[*Enter* ARTHUR L. *He is a good-looking man in the early thirties.*

ARTHUR. Hello, Mother.

MRS MARFIELD. Arthur, dear. So you managed to leave those patients of yours for a few hours to come and see your poor old mum.

ARTHUR. Peter's taken over surgery to-day. How are you, Steve?

STEPHEN. Not too bad. You look very cock-a-hoop.

ARTHUR. I've some news for you.

MRS MARFIELD. Your laboratory?

ARTHUR. Yes. We've found a place at last, and I think we can just about manage the equipment.

STEPHEN. That's fine.

MRS MARFIELD. I'm so glad. Now you can go ahead with your research work—isolating bugs, or whatever it is you do with them.

ARTHUR. It'll all have to be on a shoestring to start with. Money's the problem.

STEPHEN. It always is.

MRS MARFIELD. But can't you get help from the Government—the National Health, or something?

ARTHUR. No. We've been over all that before. You see, what we're trying to do is still in the experimental stage. It's all rather unorthodox.

STEPHEN. Even so, I think a country that spends millions on atom bombs might spend a bit more on fighting disease.

ARTHUR. We couldn't raise funds any other way; so Peter and I are paying for it ourselves.

MRS MARFIELD. Is it going to cost an awful lot?

ARTHUR. It's what I've been saving for for the past eight years.

[*Enter* JENNIFER L.

JENNIFER. Mother, there's a gentleman here from the *Sunday Globe*. He wants to see Miss Pike.

ARTHUR. Hello! What's Auntie Pie been up to?

MRS MARFIELD. You'd better show him in here, Jennifer, and I'll tell Miss Pike. [MRS MARFIELD *and* JENNIFER *go off* L.

ARTHUR. How are things at work?

STEPHEN. Much as usual.

ARTHUR. You're looking a bit under the weather. Been working too hard?

STEPHEN. No. There's nothing wrong with me. Don't start looking all professional.

JENNIFER [*at door* L.]. Just wait in here, please.

[*Enter* WALLACE L. *He is a cheerful-looking man in the thirties, with a rather self-confident manner.*

WALLACE. Good morning.

ARTHUR. Good morning.

WALLACE. Perhaps I'd better introduce myself. Wallace is the name. *Sunday Globe.*

STEPHEN. Ah, yes. You spoke to me just now on the telephone. I understand you want to see Miss Pike.

WALLACE. That's right. If I could have a little private chat with her I'd appreciate it very much.

ARTHUR. Sit down, Mr Wallace. She'll be here in a moment. [*To* STEPHEN.] Come on, we'll have a stroll round the garden, and you can tell me what you've been doing with yourself.

> [ARTHUR *and* STEPHEN *go out through french windows.*
> [*As soon as they have gone* WALLACE *rises and moves about the room, looking at everything with great interest. He picks up the newspaper. Enter* MISS PIKE L. *For a few moments they look at one another in silence.*

MISS PIKE. You want to see me?

WALLACE. Good morning. You are Miss Edith Pike?

MISS PIKE. That is my name.

WALLACE [*handing her his card*]. Mine's Wallace, and, as you see, I represent the *Sunday Globe*.

MISS PIKE. Please sit down. I can't imagine why you've come to see me.

> [*They sit facing, she in the armchair, he on the settee.*

WALLACE. Can't you, Miss Pike? [*Indicating newspaper.*] You've read of the death of Lord Dolchester?

MISS PIKE [*her nervousness increasing*]. Yes. What of it?

WALLACE. I believe you knew him many years ago.

MISS PIKE. I'm afraid there's some mistake. You must be confusing me with some one else.

WALLACE [*looking hard at her*]. I don't think so. Weren't you once known in cabaret as Clair Gilroy?

MISS PIKE. Good gracious! Whatever gave you that idea?

WALLACE. I've been trying to trace her for some time. You see, we're running a series of articles on—celebrities of the nineteen-twenties.

MISS PIKE. Celebrities? I read your account of Edith Thompson.

WALLACE. Yes. Well, in your—in Clair Gilroy's case, we very much want her life-story as told by herself. You know, the kind of personal details we can't get from the files. That's what the public go for.

MISS PIKE. Why do you want to publish it at all? It wasn't a very pretty story, was it?

WALLACE. From all accounts she was one of the most fascinating women of her time. Beauty, glamour—she had everything. And now, of course, her association with Lord Dolchester would add to public interest.

MISS PIKE. You think they'd like to wallow in all the sordid details? Can't you leave the poor woman in peace, wherever she is.

WALLACE. We'd pay well, you know. For her complete life-story we'd give as much as £5000.

MISS PIKE. Good heavens!

WALLACE. It's a tempting sum.

MISS PIKE [*rising and moving about the room*]. Why should people be interested after all these years?

WALLACE. For one thing, there was the murder case. That's always news.

MISS PIKE. Do you know what happened to her husband—I mean after he came out of prison?

WALLACE. He went to Canada. After that we lost track of him. According to the files he swore he'd kill Clair when he got out of prison. Maybe that's why she's lying low, afraid of him. She needn't be, you know. It was all talk, and, besides, Canada's a long way off.

MISS PIKE [*turning and facing him*]. I read the case years ago. Apart from this, I know nothing whatever of Clair Gilroy—so I can't help you.

WALLACE [*after a pause*]. Her real name was Pike, the same as yours.

MISS PIKE. Mine is spelt P-I-K-E. Hers was spelt with a Y.

WALLACE [*quickly*]. How do you know that?

MISS PIKE. I—I told you I read the case.

WALLACE. You have a remarkable memory for details. Weren't you a nurse at one time?

MISS PIKE. I did a little nursing years ago, but I was never fully qualified.

WALLACE. In India?

MISS PIKE. Yes.

WALLACE. So did Clair Gilroy after she left England. She also went to India. It's a strange coincidence.

MISS PIKE. It is, I'll admit. But it is only a coincidence.

WALLACE. And that's all you're going to tell me?

MISS PIKE. Listen, Mr Wallace. I heard of this woman years ago. The similarity of names struck me at the time. As far as I know, she died in India. But suppose she were still alive. She might have made a new life for herself, almost forgotten the past. Do you think it would be fair to drag her back to it, to remind every one of that horrible crime and the ghastly things that happened afterwards? What about her friends—her relatives?

WALLACE. She has no relatives, as far as we know, except, of course, the husband, Bill Holland.

MISS PIKE. What pleasure can people get out of reading of the sins and miseries of others?

WALLACE. Partly a natural interest in sex, and partly salacious piety. The Pharisee got a great kick out of checking up on the publican.

MISS PIKE [*thoughtfully*]. I could give you a story really worth publishing.

WALLACE. Yes?

MISS PIKE. Not about Clair Gilroy, but about a young doctor here in this house.

WALLACE. Indeed?

MISS PIKE. He's been working twelve—fourteen hours a day, in an East End practice, and now he's trying to open a research laboratory.

WALLACE. What's he offering? A miracle cure for something or other?

MISS PIKE. No, no, nothing like that, but he's brilliant and—something a lot of people don't understand—dedicated.

WALLACE. Not quite my cup of tea, I'm afraid. Might do for a medical journal.

MISS PIKE. Couldn't you make a story of it?

WALLACE. Afraid not. In any case doctors aren't allowed to advertise.

MISS PIKE. Oh! Why must the devil have all the limelight!

WALLACE [*smiling*]. I'm more convinced than ever that you

could tell me all I want to know about Clair. [*Taking photograph from wallet.*] I have a photograph of her here as she appeared in cabaret over thirty years ago.

[*He rises and crosses* L.C. *to show her the photograph.*

MISS PIKE. You can't possibly imagine that there's any resemblance between this woman and me.

WALLACE. I can, you know. Just now, when your eyes were flashing, I saw you exactly as you used to be. Sure you won't change your mind? Remember we'd pay quite a lot.

MISS PIKE [*rising*]. I've already told you I know nothing of Clair Gilroy except what I've read and heard.

WALLACE [*rising*]. Very well. If that's your last word I'll leave you. But in case you have second thoughts I'll give you this. [*Writes on card and hands it to her.*] My telephone number—Extension 348. Just give me a ring if you've anything to tell me, and I'll come and see you again.

MISS PIKE. Thank you, Mr Wallace, but I don't think we shall meet again.

[*She shows him out* L., *and as she does so* STEPHEN *reappears at french windows. Seeing the room empty, he comes* D.R. *to telephone, and stands looking at it. He is about to make a call, then changes his mind, and stands irresolute. He picks up the receiver, just as* ARTHUR *enters through french windows.* STEPHEN *quickly and guiltily replaces receiver.*

ARTHUR [*speaking as he enters*]. The garden's looking very well.

STEPHEN. Wish I had more time for it. I could spend hours pottering about out there but—Linda likes a social life.

ARTHUR. So I gather.

ARTHUR [*as* MISS PIKE *enters* L.]. Hello, Auntie Pie. What's all this? Reporters on your track?

MISS PIKE. It was nothing, really. He was inquiring about some one he thought I'd known in India, but it was all a mistake.

[*Her manner is nervous, and* ARTHUR *looks at her keenly.*

ARTHUR. You're a very mysterious woman, my dear.

[*Enter* LINDA R.

MISS PIKE [*to* ARTHUR]. When are you starting work in the new lab?

ARTHUR. As soon as we can get the rest of the equipment.

LINDA. Where's it going to be?

ARTHUR. Hello, Linda. Radiant as ever.

LINDA. Thanks. I said where's this new lab going to be—in Harley Street?

ARTHUR. Good lord, no! In Leytonstone.

LINDA. Where? But, my poor pet, you won't make any money there.

ARTHUR. We shan't have to spend so much either.

LINDA. In these days you have to risk money to make it. That's what I'm always telling Stephen.

STEPHEN. Can't you talk about anything else?

LINDA. No, darling, not at the moment. [*Handing letters to* STEPHEN.] These have just come by post. You'd better see them.

STEPHEN. What's all this?

LINDA. Bills.

STEPHEN [*examining them*]. Madame Milaine's—Car Hire Service—you've been hiring cars?

LINDA. I had to have something decent to go up to town in. Your old bus is a disgrace.

ARTHUR [*taking* MISS PIKE *by the arm and leading her off through french windows*]. Come on, Auntie Pie, I have a feeling we're in the way.

STEPHEN. Need you have said all that in front of Arthur?

LINDA. Just as well to let him know what we have to put up with while he's flinging money about on grand gestures.

STEPHEN. Grand gestures be damned! I envy Arthur. At least he has a purpose in life.

LINDA. You'll be telling me next that you too have a vocation—for adding up accounts in that little tin-pot office of yours.

STEPHEN. What's wrong with that?

LINDA. You're worth something better, and you could get it.

STEPHEN. How?

LINDA. How do other men get on? Look at Ferguson and Jack Carlman.

STEPHEN. I haven't Ferguson's push. As to Carlman, he's a gambler, or a financial genius. There's not much difference.

LINDA. I want to be proud of you, darling; want you to be a success.

STEPHEN. At what?

LINDA. Anything. That's up to you.

STEPHEN. I don't believe you'd care if I were running a brothel so long as it brought in enough money.

LINDA. You have a lively imagination.

STEPHEN. You knew all about my job when you married me. I told you just what I was earning.

LINDA. There is such a thing as progress. Is it unreasonable to want a home of my own?

STEPHEN. No, but we can't afford a service-flat at the Ritz.

LINDA. We could have something modern and central—the kind of place where we can invite our friends.

STEPHEN. Damn it, Linda, I'm doing my best. Can't you see I'm worried?

LINDA [*looking at him closely*]. I believe you really are. Is there something wrong? Something you haven't told me?

STEPHEN. Yes. [*Going to telephone.*] Excuse me. [*Dials.*]

LINDA. Who are you phoning?

STEPHEN [*into phone*]. Is that Mayfair 0019? Is Mr Carlman there?... This is Stephen Marfield.... Right.... Hello, Carlman. Thank heaven I've got on to you at last. I've been trying all the morning... It's about that money.... What?... But you must.... I can't possibly wait. Don't you understand?... Look, I explained the whole thing to you, and you promised—gave me your solemn word.... Yes.... Look, can I come over and see you, or will you come here?... No, that'll be too late.... Carlman, you *must* help me. You—— Hello, hello.... [*Replaces receiver.*] Oh, my God!

LINDA. What is it?

STEPHEN. I'm in a mess, Linda. I've done something stupid.
[*Sits on settee.*]

LINDA. Tell me. [ARTHUR *enters through french windows.*]

ARTHUR. Am I interrupting anything?

STEPHEN. No, no, Arthur.

LINDA. Steve's got into some sort of mess, and he won't tell me what it is.

ARTHUR. What's up, old chap? Can I help?

STEPHEN [*rising*]. I'm going over to see Carlman right away.

L

ARTHUR. Carlman? Do you mean Jack Carlman, the fellow you were telling me about last week?

STEPHEN. Yes. I'll make him give me back that money.

ARTHUR. Money? If you've lent him any I don't think you'll see it again.

LINDA. What do you know about Jack?

ARTHUR. Plenty. I've been making a few inquiries.

STEPHEN [*going to door* L.]. I'll get it if I have to choke it out of him.

ARTHUR [*seizing him by the arm*]. Here, hold on a minute. You'll only make things worse.

STEPHEN. They couldn't be.

ARTHUR [*bringing him* D.L.C. *to armchair*]. You'd better sit down there and tell me what this is all about.

STEPHEN. It all started a few weeks ago at that party. [*To* LINDA.] You remember we were talking about wanting to buy a house, and Carlman said he could help me.

ARTHUR. How?

STEPHEN. He said I could be a sort of partner in one of his property deals. He was on to a good thing, and if I could only raise two thousand pounds, in a few months I could double my capital.

LINDA. Where could you get two thousand pounds?

STEPHEN. I told him I hadn't a bean, and he said he'd lend it to me himself—only at the moment his own capital was all tied up.

ARTHUR. Well?

STEPHEN. He kept talking about it, saying what a good thing I was missing, and then he said that if only I could raise the cash till the end of the month he'd let me have it back—as a personal loan—and I could still be in the deal.

ARTHUR. Didn't you wonder why he was being so kind?

STEPHEN. I thought he needed the ready money.

LINDA. But he's rolling.

STEPHEN. Yes, but it's all invested.

LINDA. Two thousand pounds means nothing to him.

STEPHEN. Anyway, it was to be a business arrangement. I'd have paid him interest, of course.

ARTHUR. So what did you do?

STEPHEN. I tried to borrow the money, but there was nothing doing.

ARTHUR. And then? Come on, old chap, you'd better tell me the worst.

STEPHEN. I—took it from the firm.

ARTHUR. You what?

LINDA. Stephen, you fool.

ARTHUR [*to* LINDA]. Shut up. You're as much to blame for this as he is.

STEPHEN. I thought I'd have plenty of time to put it back. Carlman gave me his solemn oath——

ARTHUR. That's worth nothing. How long before the money'll be missed?

STEPHEN. They'll know at the end of the month, when the auditors come in.

ARTHUR. That's next week.

STEPHEN. Yes.

ARTHUR. Does Carlman know you took the money?

STEPHEN. Yes, and he swore he'd give it back to me in time.

ARTHUR. Well, he won't.

LINDA [*to* ARTHUR]. You seem to know a mighty lot about it.

ARTHUR. Don't you know how Carlman's been getting rich?

LINDA. In some sort of speculation.

ARTHUR. Buying up old houses with controlled rents, getting the tenants out—by any foul means—and then letting single rooms to prostitutes.

LINDA. I don't believe it.

ARTHUR. No? When people talk about doubling their capital in a few months what do you think they're doing—going to work every day at union rates?

STEPHEN [*to* ARTHUR]. Do you *know* all this, or are you just guessing?

ARTHUR. I *know*, Steve. Some of the houses are in my district.

LINDA. But he's got plenty, so why can't he pay back the two thousand?

ARTHUR. You still don't care where it comes from, do you?

LINDA. I'm thinking of Stephen. Do you want him to go to prison?

ARTHUR. That's where Carlman will be before long. He went too far with some of his poor old tenants. They wouldn't get out, so he had them beaten up. They went to the police.

STEPHEN. When did all this happen?

ARTHUR. A few days ago. It will be in the papers soon. The police and the local council are on to him now. So you see Carlman's racket is exploded.

LINDA. God!

STEPHEN [*quietly*]. Then—I'm finished. There's nothing I can do.

ARTHUR [*after a pause*]. If you had the money to-morrow could you put it back without anyone knowing?

STEPHEN. Yes, but where am I going to get a sum like that?

ARTHUR. I'll let you have it.

STEPHEN. You?

LINDA. Arthur, darling, would you really do that for us.

ARTHUR. I'm doing it for my brother.

STEPHEN. But—it's the money you've been saving for your lab.

ARTHUR. That'll have to wait for a bit.

[JENNIFER *appears at door* L.

JENNIFER. Lunch is nearly ready. Mother's going to dish up.

LINDA. All right, Jennifer, we shan't be a minute. Run along.

[JENNIFER, *sensing that something is afoot, lingers in the doorway.*

STEPHEN [*to* ARTHUR]. I can't let you do this.

ARTHUR. Don't be a fool, man, you've got to.

STEPHEN. But it means the end of all your own plans.

ARTHUR. They can wait. If I give you a cheque to-night can you cash it to-morrow and put things right?

STEPHEN. I'll pay you back, Arthur, just as soon as I can.

ARTHUR. We'll talk about that later.

LINDA [*to* ARTHUR]. You're being wonderful. We'll neither of us ever forget it.

ARTHUR. I think we'll skip all that. There's just one thing I want you to promise me—both of you.

STEPHEN. Yes?

ARTHUR. Not a word about this to Mother. Understand?

STEPHEN. Of course.

ARTHUR [*going to writing-table and getting out cheque book*]. I'll make out the cheque.

[*He hurriedly conceals it as* MRS MARFIELD *enters* L.

MRS MARFIELD [*going to table* U.R.C.]. Lunch is ready, but before we have it I think we all deserve a drink.

ARTHUR. That's a good idea.

MRS MARFIELD [*pouring drinks*]. This is something of an occasion. We'll drink to Arthur's success.

ARTHUR. I'm not going in orbit round the moon, you know.

MRS MARFIELD. No, but you're starting a new venture—something you've been looking forward to for years. And I dare say it will do a lot more good than flying around in space.

ARTHUR. Let's hope so.

MRS MARFIELD. You like gin-and-orange, don't you, Linda? And you, Arthur. Sherry for you, Stephen?

STEPHEN. Thanks, Mother.

MRS MARFIELD. Orange for Jenny, and—where's Miss Pike? She must be in this.

LINDA [*going to door* L. *and calling*]. Miss Pike. Jenny.

[MISS PIKE *and* JENNIFER *enter* L. *and* MRS MARFIELD *hands them glasses.*

MRS MARFIELD. There you are. [*Holding up her glass.*] Here's good health to every one, and, Arthur dear—all success.

ARTHUR. Thanks. Cheers, every one. [*They drink.*

MRS MARFIELD. Oh, by the way, while I think of it—I hope you're all free next Sunday—to-morrow week. I promised we'd go to Uncle George's.

ARTHUR. Righto.

LINDA. Count us out, please. Stephen and I have fixed up something else.

MRS MARFIELD. Very well, Linda.

JENNIFER [*finishing her drink*]. H'm. That was good stuff. Can I have a drop of gin in it?

MRS MARFIELD. No, you can't. Come along now, and have your lunch.

[*They all go off* L. *except* MISS PIKE *and* ARTHUR.

MISS PIKE. One moment, Arthur.

ARTHUR. Yes?

MISS PIKE. Jennifer overheard something just now—about that money.

ARTHUR. Good Lord! She hasn't said anything to Mother?

MISS PIKE. No. I warned her not to, but she blurted it all out to me.

ARTHUR. I know I can trust you to keep your mouth shut.

MISS PIKE. Of course. But what's going to happen about the lab?

ARTHUR. I'll have to tell Peter it's all off for the time being.

MISS PIKE. I'm sorry.

ARTHUR. Thanks. But don't show it, please, and do something to stop that terrible child from talking. [*After a pause.*] Come on, Auntie Pie, don't look so down in the mouth. It's not the end of the world, you know.   [*They go off* L.

[*After a moment* MISS PIKE *returns.*]

MISS PIKE [*as she re-enters*]. Just a moment. I think I left my bag in here.

[*She goes to writing-table and takes the card from her bag. For a few moments she stands staring at it, then lifts telephone receiver and dials a number.*]

MISS PIKE [*into phone*]. Is that the *Sunday Globe*? I want extension 348.... May I speak to Mr Wallace, please? Thank you.... Hello, Mr Wallace. This is Miss Pike speaking.... I've thought things over and decided to let you have that story.... Yes, of course, you were quite right. I am Clair Gilroy.

The CURTAIN *falls slowly.*

SCENE II: *The same. Three hours later. At rise of curtain* MISS PIKE *is discovered sitting on settee.* WALLACE *sits opposite to her in the armchair. He is taking notes.*

WALLACE. Now, I should like a little more about your early life, especially your first meeting with Bill Holland. [*Checking his notes.*] You've told me about your parents and your schooldays. You had only one sister, and I gather you weren't very good friends with her.

MISS PIKE. Perhaps I was jealous of Barbara. I thought she had more affection from our parents. Anyhow, we were poles apart.

I always thought her rather a prig—what they call nowadays a "do-gooder."

WALLACE. And when did you first meet Bill Holland?

MISS PIKE. In 1917. It was one night when a crowd of us had been to see *Chu-Chin-Chow*. Bill was an officer in the Royal Artillery. He was very gay and handsome in those days. I just fell in love with him right away.

WALLACE. And he with you?

MISS PIKE. Not at first. He was Barbara's friend. I think he'd have married her but for me. I was determined to have him myself. [*After a pause.*] That shocks you, doesn't it?

WALLACE. Not at all. You were in love with him.

MISS PIKE. I suppose that's some excuse. That, and the crazy times we were living in.

WALLACE. I understand.

MISS PIKE. You don't, because you weren't even born then. You can't begin to understand how the world completely changed during those mad years of the First World War. Everything we'd believed in—honour, integrity—became a kind of joke. To be chaste was to be ungenerous; one must give and enjoy to-night, because to-morrow might be too late. We dropped a long way in those years, and we've never climbed back.

WALLACE. You were telling me about Bill.

MISS PIKE. Yes. I didn't care what I did to get him. One evening in 1918 he came home on leave unexpectedly. He tried to phone Barbara, but I took the message and told her nothing about it. She was visiting an aunt who was very ill at the time, but I told Bill she was with another man. He spent his leave with me.

WALLACE. And did you—? Were you—?

MISS PIKE. You want to know it all, don't you? Yes, we were lovers. Later I let Barbara know what had happened, but not about the lies I'd told Bill. Poor Barbara was always a bit of a fool, and, you see, she had a pre-War mind. She thought Bill ought to marry me, and just went away without giving him a chance to explain.

WALLACE. When were you married?

MISS PIKE. Just before the end of the War. We spent our honeymoon in Eastbourne. I remember it so well. The place was full of wounded soldiers, in blue. We got so depressed we came back to town and stayed for a week at the Savoy.

WALLACE. You were happy together?

MISS PIKE. Oh, yes. For the first few months it was heaven. Then Bill had spent his gratuity, and found himself out of a job.

WALLACE. Were you working then?

MISS PIKE. Yes, in small cabaret shows, but not earning very much.

WALLACE. How did Bill feel about that?

MISS PIKE. He hated it. He started getting jealous of every man I met, and we had frightful rows.

WALLACE. And then?

MISS PIKE. Then I met Eddie Clynes. He offered me a job at the Blue Parrot, and I jumped at it. Bill was furious—swore I was sleeping with Eddie. Actually I wasn't—at that time.

WALLACE. Why did your husband kill Clynes?

MISS PIKE. You know all that.

WALLACE. Yes, but I want your own story.

MISS PIKE. I was grateful to Eddie. He'd helped me at a time when things were very bad, so I gave him what he wanted.

WALLACE. Were you in love with him?

MISS PIKE. Of course not. Virtue had become just a coin of gratitude. I used to go to his flat in the afternoons, and told Bill I was going to rehearsals. One day he followed me. I've never understood quite how he got in. Eddie's door must have been unlatched, because suddenly Bill was there in the room. It was horrible.

WALLACE. What happened?

MISS PIKE. Eddie made things worse. He said something about a man who couldn't keep his wife, and at that Bill went raving mad. He grabbed a heavy brass ornament from a shelf and struck Eddie over the head. I don't remember very clearly what happened after that, except that I stood there saying, "You've killed him," and Bill said, "I killed better men in the War." Then a janitor came and brought the police. Bill was charged with murder.

WALLACE. How did you feel when you were giving evidence at his trial?

MISS PIKE. What could I feel but misery and shame?

WALLACE. Bill said you didn't tell the whole truth.

MISS PIKE. I couldn't. Oh, I didn't commit perjury or anything like that, but with all those eyes leering at me—somehow, I just couldn't put it all into words.

WALLACE. That was very understandable.

MISS PIKE. But if I had I might have saved him; at least he'd have got a lighter sentence.

WALLACE. Oh, I don't know. This isn't France. We don't recognize the *crime passionel*.

MISS PIKE. Bill thought I could have saved him. That's why, after he'd been sentenced, he swore he'd kill me.

WALLACE. That was just the heat of the moment. He's forgotten it long ago.

MISS PIKE. Would you forget if some one sent you to prison for fifteen years?

WALLACE. What did you do after the trial?

MISS PIKE. Went through a hell of remorse.

WALLACE. And then?

MISS PIKE. I tried to kill it in the usual ways—drink and drugs.

WALLACE. But you were a great success in the night-club world.

MISS PIKE. Oh, yes. My notoriety helped enormously. I was earning fabulous money.

WALLACE. And then you met Lord Dolchester.

MISS PIKE. That lasted until he found out about the drugs. He persuaded me to go into a nursing-home.

WALLACE. Yes, well, I think we've covered all that. These "cures" never lasted?

MISS PIKE. By 1930 I was just about finished. Things were desperate. They must have been or I wouldn't have written to Barbara.

WALLACE. You'd kept in touch with her?

MISS PIKE. No, but I found her through the Red Cross. She'd gone out to India with a medical mission, but as soon as she got my letter she came back to help me.

WALLACE. That was good of her.

MISS PIKE. I suppose it was. But I think she got a kind of kick out of it. You know, the Good Samaritan. She took me back to India, and tried to teach me nursing so that I could help at the mission. I wasn't a great success.

WALLACE. But you stuck it?

MISS PIKE. Yes, until my sister died. I came home in '47, drifted around in lodging-houses for a while. Then I came here.

WALLACE. Thank you very much. You've been most helpful. We'll let you have a proof of this, of course.

MISS PIKE. I dread to think what will happen when the paper comes into this house. I shall have to go,of course. I can just imagine them reading it.

[*During this speech the* CURTAIN *slowly falls. It rises again almost immediately on:*]

SCENE III: *The same. Eight days later. It is early evening.* MRS MARFIELD, *in armchair* L.C., *is studying a copy of the "Sunday Globe."* JENNIFER *has another copy spread out on the writing-table, and* LINDA *is looking over her shoulder.* ARTHUR *is moving restlessly about the room, and* STEPHEN *is at table of drinks.*

MRS MARFIELD. I still can't believe it. Miss Pike! Our Miss Pike!

LINDA [*moving* U.R.C. *and taking drink from Stephen*]. I always said she was a dark horse.

JENNIFER. You didn't. You said she was a dull old toad.

STEPHEN. Where is she, by the way?

MRS MARFIELD. Up in her room. She's been there nearly all day.

LINDA. Ashamed to face us, perhaps.

ARTHUR. What beats me is why she let them publish it.

LINDA. Money, of course. She must have made a packet out of this.

JENNIFER [*looking at pictures*]. She's got smashing legs in this one. "Clair Gilroy as she appeared at the Blue Parrot in 1928." Gosh! Is that really Auntie Pie?

MRS MARFIELD. You'd better put those papers away.

JENNIFER. But I didn't think people did things like that in those days.

STEPHEN. What days?

JENNIFER. Mother's young days. I thought it was only us—

STEPHEN. What do they teach you for history?

JENNIFER [*rising and going to french window*]. Oh, history! Yes. That's different. Charles the Second, and all that!

STEPHEN. You thought we'd had three hundred years of unblemished virtue until you came along to spoil it.

MRS MARFIELD. I suppose she'll be getting a lot of letters.

ARTHUR. Sure to. People have been ringing up already.

LINDA. Who?

ARTHUR. A lot of cranks.

JENNIFER. I say, there's a man outside, watching the house.

ARTHUR [*hurrying to window*]. Where?

JENNIFER. He's gone now. He went round the corner, but he's been there for hours.

STEPHEN. Probably one of your boy-friends.

JENNIFER. Don't be soppy. He's an old man. He keeps walking away, then coming back, and looking at the window.

MRS MARFIELD. Oh, dear. I don't like the sound of this. We've never had a scandal here, and now—

[MISS PIKE *enters* R. *They all look at her, and there is an awkward silence.*]

MISS PIKE. Am I intruding?

STEPHEN [*embarrassed*]. Of course not.

MISS PIKE [*going quietly to settee*]. I think I left my knitting in here.

[*She sits on settee, and goes quietly on with her knitting. The others look at one another, then from the newspapers to* MISS PIKE. *They are overwhelmed by the contrast.* ARTHUR *comes* D.R.C., *looking at* MISS PIKE, *then he bursts into a quiet chuckle.*]

ARTHUR. You certainly were quite a girl, Auntie Pie.

[*He puts his arm round her, and kisses her heartily on the cheek.*]

MISS PIKE. Thank you, Arthur dear. [*Looking round at the others.*] I suppose you've all read it.

LINDA. We couldn't very well miss it, could we?

MISS PIKE. I shall be leaving here during the week.

MRS MARFIELD. Oh, no!

STEPHEN. Good heavens! Why?

MISS PIKE. I know how unpleasant it would be for you all if I stayed.

ARTHUR. Nonsense. You can't go after all these years. You're one of the family.

MISS PIKE. That's why I'm going. If I were just an ordinary lodger it wouldn't matter so much. Besides, I want to find another hiding-place.

MRS MARFIELD. It just doesn't seem possible! I mean—you, of all people! Tell me——

MISS PIKE. Won't you be late for Uncle George's?

MRS MARFIELD [*rising*]. Oh, yes. I'd forgotten we were going. Are you coming with us?

MISS PIKE. If you'll excuse me I'd rather not.

MRS MARFIELD. You were invited. You know they're always pleased to see you.

MISS PIKE. Perhaps not to-night.

LINDA. We'll have to be getting along too, Stephen, or we'll be late for the Fergusons'.

STEPHEN [*going out through french window*]. Right. I'll get the car out.

LINDA [*going off* L. *with newspaper*]. I'm longing to see their faces. They'll be tickled pink about this.

MRS MARFIELD. You'd better get your coat on, Jennifer.

JENNIFER. O.K. [*At door* L. *to* MISS PIKE.] I say, will you sign my autograph-book before you go?

MRS MARFIELD. Go along, Jennifer.   [JENNIFER *goes off* L. [*To* MISS PIKE.] I don't like leaving you here alone.

MISS PIKE. That's quite all right. I have plenty of things to do.

MRS MARFIELD [*at door* L.]. Very well, if that's what you prefer.

[*She is about to go, hesitates, then comes impulsively* D.R.C. *to* MISS PIKE.

Good night, my dear. I— [*turning away almost in tears*] oh—I wish we still didn't know about all this.   [*She hurries off* L.

ARTHUR [*sitting beside* MISS PIKE *on settee*]. Why did you let them publish it?

MISS PIKE. I wanted the money.

ARTHUR. That doesn't sound like you.

MISS PIKE. They paid me quite a lot because, you see, it was a personal confession they wanted. They say the public like it that way. It makes them feel as if they really know my thoughts, almost as though they're living it all themselves.

ARTHUR. You must have wanted that money very badly.

MISS PIKE. Yes, I'd a special reason. [*Taking a cheque from her bag.*] I want you to do something for me. I want you to take this cheque.

ARTHUR [*looking at it in amazement*]. Five thousand pounds!

MISS PIKE. That's what they paid me. I want you to use it for your new lab.

ARTHUR [*rising*]. I wouldn't dream of such a thing.

MISS PIKE. Please, Arthur, as a favour to me. It will buy all the equipment you need, and it will give me so much happiness to think I'm doing some good at last.

ARTHUR. I couldn't take your money.

MISS PIKE. You mean ... it's tainted?

ARTHUR. No. I never thought of anything like that.

MISS PIKE. Then please take it for my sake. I've always believed in your work. I know you're going to do something splendid, perhaps find a cure that will save lives. Don't you see, if I could have a part in it, feel that I'd helped, it would make up for so much that I'm sorry for.

ARTHUR. How can I possibly take all this money from you?

MISS PIKE. It's not really from me. In a way it's from the newspaper. I tried to get that reporter interested in your work. I thought the right kind of publicity might help. But it was only my sordid story they wanted. There's no glamour for the good.

ARTHUR. And you let them pillory you just to help me?

MISS PIKE. To help your work. Don't you see it's my one chance of doing something decent? So much of my life has been a failure. Don't let me fail in this.

ARTHUR. If I take it everything will have to be in your name.

MISS PIKE. Names don't matter. It's the job.

ARTHUR. Then what can I say except thank you and God bless you.

MISS PIKE. You've made me very happy.

ARTHUR. But you're not to think of leaving here.

MISS PIKE. I must. For your mother's sake and Jennifer's. Now that she knows my story I shouldn't be a good influence.

ARTHUR. Nonsense.

MISS PIKE. No.

ARTHUR. Where would you go?

MISS PIKE. I'll find somewhere quiet where I can be unknown again.

ARTHUR. This place won't be the same without you.

MISS PIKE. I'll be sorry, too. You've all been so kind, and this has been my home. Somehow, I always thought I should end my days here.

ARTHUR. Now don't start talking like that. You're good for donkey's years.

MISS PIKE [*with a smile*]. I hope that's a true medical opinion.

MRS MARFIELD [*off* L.]. Are you coming, Arthur?

ARTHUR [*calling*]. Righto, Mother. [*To* MISS PIKE.] I must go. We'll be home as early as we can. Sure you'll be all right?

MISS PIKE. Quite sure. Good night, Arthur.

[*As he goes off* L. *she whispers "Goodbye."*
[*When he has gone she goes to writing-table and stands for a few minutes looking at the newspaper. She shudders as if at a painful memory. An outer door is heard to close off* L. *There follows the sound of a car starting up and leaving.* MISS PIKE *collects a few small possessions, papers, books, needlework, etc., and packs them into a large holdall. There is a ring at the door-bell off* L. *She stands listening. It is repeated. She goes off* L. *and there is the sound of an outer door opening.*

MAN'S VOICE [*off* L.]. Is it Miss Pike?

MISS PIKE [*off* L.]. Yes.

MAN'S VOICE [*off*]. I'll come in if you don't mind.

[*Sound of outer door being sharply closed.*

MISS PIKE [*off*]. Who are you? What do you want?

MAN'S VOICE [*off*]. A little talk with you.

[*Re-enter* MISS PIKE *followed by* BILL HOLLAND. *He is tall, slim, and still a handsome man, despite his sixty years.*

His hair is nearly white, and there are lines of suffering in his face, but he has a look of strength and almost fanatical resolution.

MISS PIKE [*speaking as she enters*]. Come in, then. What do you want to see me about?

BILL [*staring at her*]. Well, well! So you're Clair. Don't you know me?

MISS PIKE [*recognizing him and speaking in a whisper*]. Bill!

BILL. Yes, it's Bill—your long-forgotten husband. You didn't expect to see me again, did you?

MISS PIKE. I thought you were in Canada.

BILL. I have been, but how did you know?

MISS PIKE. Some one told me.

BILL. Who?

MISS PIKE. A reporter.

BILL. Ah, yes, of course. [*Indicating newspaper.*] I read your remarkable confessions this morning. You can imagine with what interest. I lost no time in finding you. It wasn't difficult.

MISS PIKE [*still rather dazed*]. Won't you sit down?

BILL. And have a drink with you, perhaps? No, thanks.

MISS PIKE. I was going to offer you one.

BILL. What I have to say can be said standing, and I don't need drink to help me say it.

MISS PIKE. Well? What is it?

BILL [*after a pause*]. You've no shame, even now, have you? No remorse for what you did to me?

MISS PIKE. You're wrong.

BILL. Don't lie. You're proud of yourself, so proud that you had to smear this all over the Gutter Press.

MISS PIKE. I needed the money.

BILL. You haven't changed so much, have you? You were always ready to sell your body and soul.

MISS PIKE. You don't understand. It wasn't for myself——

BILL. I suppose they paid you well.

MISS PIKE. I'd gladly give you every penny of it, but——

BILL. Is that what you think? Do you suppose I came here for money?

MISS PIKE. Why did you come?

BILL. Because I took an oath a long time ago. Have you forgotten?

MISS PIKE. What do you mean?

BILL. Think, Clair. Have you ever thought what it's like when those doors close behind you for fifteen years? Fifteen years of living death, and it was you who sent me there.

MISS PIKE. *I* couldn't have saved you.

BILL. Of course you could. Do you think they'd have given me "life" if you'd told the whole story? But that would have spoilt your chances, wouldn't it? You'd met Lord Dolchester by then, and you didn't want him to know what a dirty little slut you were.

MISS PIKE. It's all so long ago. Can't you try to forgive?

BILL. Forgive! Do you know what? I think I might have forgiven you even that if I hadn't read those confessions.

MISS PIKE. I don't understand.

BILL. This morning I learned for the first time just what you really did to me. You lied from the start. It was you who parted me from Barbara—a woman as good and fine as you are damned to hell.

MISS PIKE. That's not true.

BILL. Listen Clair, you're an old woman now, but you may as well know the truth. What I felt for you all those years ago was lust, desire—call it what you like—but it was never love. Your sister was the only woman I ever really loved.

[*She smiles, and this infuriates him.*

BILL. So that amuses you, does it? It makes you happy to think how clever you were, how you spoilt her life just as you ruined mine [*approaching her as though about to seize her by the throat*]. By God, I'll wipe that smile off your face if I——

MISS PIKE [*almost shouting at him*]. Bill! What's happened to you? Are you blind? [*Quietly.*] Look at me, Bill. Look at me.

[*He stops short, staring at her incredulously.*

BILL [*slowly*]. You're—you're *not* Clair.

MISS PIKE [*quietly*]. Clair died years ago in India.

BILL [*a light of recognition and joy breaking over his face*]. You —why—you're *BARBARA*.

The CURTAIN *falls.*